THE BOOK OF

Love

PASTOR RON SWINGLE

iUniverse, Inc.

New York   Bloomington

The Book Of Love

iUniverse books may be ordered through booksellers or by contacting:

iUniverse
1663 Liberty Drive
Bloomington, IN 47403
www.iuniverse.com
1-800-Authors (1-800-288-4677)

ISBN: 978-1-4502-2894-7 (pbk)
ISBN: 978-1-4502-2895-4 (ebook)

Printed in the United States of America

iUniverse rev. date: 6/4/10

DEDICATION

To Pastor Tom Schaller:

My Pastor,
my teacher,
my intercessor,
my best friend in Christ;
A model of Love to many.

ACKNOWLEDGMENTS

Margie:

My faithful wife;
        for her fervent
        prayers,
                her continuing support,
                and her relentless
                encouragement.

Melissa Quickel:

My sister in the Lord;
        for her encouragement,
        prayers,
        patience,
        and labor of love
        in transcribing Pastor
        Schaller's messages.

TABLE OF CONTENTS

FORWARD

Pastor Tom Schaller is the overseeing pastor of Greater Grace World Outreach Ministries, based in Baltimore, MD. On a flight to Budapest, Hungary, to head up our *European Convention (Eurocon),* he read a paper about *"Love"* by Charles Finney, and was so deeply touched by it that he decided to use "Love" for the 2007 Eurocon theme. Everyone present at the convention was blessed by every message. As he reflected upon the enormous success of the convention during his return flight, Pastor Schaller knew he had to continue this magnificent theme with a series of messages at his home church.

I must say: I was profoundly inspired by that series. Every message brought tears to my eyes; every word touched my heart, every thought brought peace to my soul, an entirely new perspective on "love" became a life-changing experience for me; I knew I had been touched by His love. And I was not aware of it at the time, but I now know that God was systematically preparing me for the writing of my first book, "The Book of Love", a compilation of excerpts of ten anointed messages preached by Pastor Schaller, in addition to much revelation and commentary they inspired in me personally.

I humbly present this book to you with a prayer that you, also, will be...touched by Love, because:

God loves YOU
—whoever you are—
very, very, very much!

Please Note: All scriptures are quoted from the New King James Version (NKJV) unless otherwise specified.

Chapter 1
– Victory Because of Love –

Introduction: The Channel Of Charity

And above all things have fervent love for one another, for "love will cover a multitude of sins." Be hospitable to one another without grumbling. As each one has received a gift, minister it to one another, as good stewards of the manifold grace of God.

1 Peter 10:8-10

I'm so very grateful to God for our Church, for every Christian Brother and Sister, and for the Body of Christ everywhere, because these are God's chosen channels of *charity* [Greek: *agape*, divine love], [1Co 13] ministering stewards of His grace [1Pe 4:10] and His love. [He 6:10] We could say that the essence of grace is the manifestation of divine love; we can see this by many ways and means but nowhere is it more obvious than in and through the Body of Christ.

Pr. Tom Schaller:

On the flight over to our 2006 Budapest Conference, I read a sermon on, *Agape* Love, preached by Charles Finney in 1849, and was so deeply touched that I decided to use this subject matter for our conference theme. Everyone was blessed by every message, every service was well attended, and our fellowship during and after each service, and at every meeting, was rich with insight and revelation. I felt that I already had a good understanding of *agape* because I have

1

studied it and, by grace, I do live in it every day as best I know how, but we all learned something at this conference: If anyone thinks that he knows anything, he knows nothing yet as he ought to know. (1Co 8:2)

On the return flight, there were many new thoughts and precious memories to meditate upon. In addition to messages already shared at the conference (other's as well as my own) several more were inspired.

It was this theme and the Love we all experience from Heaven daily through the Body of Christ on earth that ultimately gave birth to this book.

Of all the doctrines in the Bible, God's love is one of the most profound by its impact upon every area of life (Christian or otherwise) because love is a need fundamental and essential to our total being—body, soul, and spirit.

In the ancient Garden of Eden we lost something that would seal our fate forever, the innate, uninhibited ability to freely receive and give the love of God. But the Son of His love supernaturally intervened in the affairs of fallen mankind to redeem all who trust in Him as Savior. The instant we believe, we are raised-up and made to sit together with Him in Heavenly places, that in ages to come He might reveal to us the immeasurable riches of His love. (Ep 2:6-7)

I am persuaded that the love of God is the prominent theme of the Bible. Only the entirety of God's Word enduring to all generations (Ps 100:5) can even begin to communicate the depths of Love, and it will literally take all of Heaven and eternity to totally reveal it. When we've been in Heaven for a sqillion years we will still be learning about *agape*.

> *If I would call the Bible*
> *by any other name,*
> *it must be... "The Book Of Love".*

1

The Gift of Love

> Though I speak with the tongues of men and of angels, but have not love, I have become sounding brass or a clanging cymbal.

> 1 Corinthians 13:1

In the New King James Bible (NKJV) "love" is interpreted from the Greek, *agape*, meaning a special, unique form of love. The King James Bible (KJV) calls it *"charity"* to delineate that great truth, and distinguish it from all other forms of the word. *Charity*, or *agape*, is divine love: love that is intrinsic in God's very character and nature, [1Jo 4:8,16] the highest possible form of love, perfect love in the absolute sense of the word. 1 Corinthians 13, The great Love chapter of the Bible, begins with a note of caution concerning words because they are so very important to communicating love.

> Let no foul or polluting language, nor evil word nor unwholesome or worthless talk [ever] come out of your mouth, but only such [speech] as is good and beneficial to the spiritual progress of others, as is fitting to the need and the occasion, that it may be a blessing and give grace (God's favor) to those who hear it.

> Ephesians 4:29

Every word we speak should have its source in *agape* love even as God's Word totally and absolutely does.

Most of the time we have no idea how our words sound to others, or how foolish we look in Heaven's eyes when our tongue has its unbridled way. [Ja 3:8] I know of a very intelligent man who speaks several languages fluently. He has a lot to say about a lot of things, and he is a skillful communicator, but he's incapable of communicating God's love because he knows nothing of it himself. As far as Heaven is concerned all the words of this man, no matter how eloquent they may be to the ears of the world, are as sounding brass—annoying noise, no less! The phrase used by the Amplified Bible is "as a noisy gong". When he speaks, the world hears the words of a gifted orator, but God hears this: Gong, gong::: clang::: gong-gong-gong :::gong...gong ::: clang::: gong-gong, and He places his hands over his ears. As I look back over my last sentence it's even ridiculous and annoying to read it!

It's amazing how deceived we can be about how talented we are, especially when it comes to singing? As I watched the tryouts for *American Idol* (A popular, amateur singing competition on national TV) at times I felt sorry for some who were not chosen—did not make the cut—for the actual competition. They really did put forth a tremendous effort but they just didn't seem to have what it takes, and most of them were very humble in receiving the bad news, but there were some who were as sounding brass, untalented wannabes, and they were totally shocked and offended that they weren't chosen. Their audacity before the judges as they got the bad news was laughable. And their speech revealed their love—not Love—but love of self. If you've ever watched this show you know exactly what I mean.

Many are naturally gifted and talented but lack this singular thing that makes a gift truly spiritual and a joy for the Body of Christ to experience: Love. Without Love anything we have to offer is as sounding brass; off key, out-of-harmony with the plan and purpose of the Gift Giver, which is to glorify Him before all of Heaven and earth.

But let's consider a *Heavenly* Idol competition; believers participate in it every day of their life. A great cloud of witnesses [He 12:1-2] is tuned-in to Planet Earth, eagerly watching and waiting to see who the winners will be. And I'm sure that, even though it actually is very serious business, they often have a good belly laugh at the sounding brass and tinkling cymbals of humanity trying very hard to be spiritual while they have not Love.

Now I know I'm not much of a singer—almost always off-key—but I sing at every service in response to Love in our midst; God is glorified, the Body of Christ is edified, and this is all that really matters because this is the purpose of all spiritual gifts. If I have not charity, I am nothing, but if I do have charity, by the grace of God, I am what I am [1Co 15:10] ...even an awesome, spiritual singer!

> Words are things of little cost,
> Quickly spoken, quickly lost;
> We forget them, but they stand,
> Witness at God's right hand.
>
> Grant us, Lord, from day to day,
> Strength to watch, and grace to pray;
> May our lips, from sin set free,
> Love to speak and sing to thee.

C.H. Spurgeon

Love is the gift essential to all gifts.

1

Perfected Love

No man has at any time yet seen God, but if we love one another, God abides (lives and remains) in us and His love (that which is essentially His) is brought to completion (to full maturity, runs it's full course, is perfected) in us!

And we know (understand, recognize, are conscious of, by observation and by experience) and believe (adhere to and put faith in and rely on) the love God cherishes for us. God is love, and he who dwells and continues in love dwells and continues in God and God dwells and continues in him. In this [union and communion with him] love is brought to completion and attains perfection with us that we may have confidence for the day of judgment [with assurance and boldness to face Him], because as He is, so are we in this world...

1John 4:12, 16-17 (Amplified)

Needless to say, human love is anything but perfect. But divine love is *perfect* love and is the very nature of God who *is* love; [1Jn 4:8,16] I often define this love with capitalization (Love). Now, divine love (*agape*) is the highest form of love, but divine love working through human love (*phileo*) is the highest manifestation of love, or Love "brought to completion" and "perfected in us". In other words, perfect, divine Love manifested through imperfect, human love becomes *perfected* Love [1Jn 4:12]—a singular form of love made possible when Jesus Christ made his soul to be an offering for sin; [Is 53:10] and God made him who knew no sin to be sin for us, that we might become the righteousness of God in him. [2Co 5:21] This glorious event—the Crucifixion of the Lord Jesus Christ—opened the way for the New Covenant, the Grace

Dispensation, the indwelling of Christ in every believer, (Ep 3:17, Co 1:27) and also his/her filling and sealing of the Holy Spirit. (Ac 2:4)

Perfected Love is the very thing that angels "desire to look into". (1Pe 1:12) When God created them the first thing ever their eyes did see was the face of Perfect Love. Astonished and overwhelmed with His beauty from the first instant of their existence, they knew Love to be absolutely supreme. But they had not yet seen *perfected* Love; that would be revealed in the sinless Christ when he became our sin on the Cross. Angels were amazed when the likes of Abraham, Isaac, Jacob, David and many others would believe and receive a new heart filled with Love; they knew the mystery of it but—like Daniel—for them full understanding was shut-up and sealed, (Dn 12:4) hidden. (1Co 2:7) Now it is revealed! (Co 1:27) Now, as they protect and minister to us (Ps 34:7, 1Pe 3:22) they rejoice (Lu 15:10) knowing that they too have the privilege of participating in some way, in a ministry of perfected Love, and they do so with the greatest of zeal.

Many Christians in this age of grace do not understand that, while God loves everyone, His love alone cannot save anyone; only His love expressed through His sinless Son, dying on the Cross could do that. As perfect as God's love is, only *perfected* Love could ever do that... and it did! In eternity all of the history of creation, and all of the testimony of all the saints and angels will finally focus upon one profound thing: the unsearchable riches of grace manifested in perfected Love. (Ep 3:8)

In the history of creation
there is nothing comparable to the beauty,
and the wonder of perfect Love,
working through imperfect love,
to manifest perfected Love!

1

Quality Love

The Disciples were very discouraged, to say the least, by the crucifixion and death of Jesus, but his resurrection and personal appearance in a glorified, human body, should have encouraged them. How could it be that so soon after his second appearance Peter abruptly chucked it all and went back to his nets, taking many of the others with him? We surmise that it might be because they were not yet Spirit filled believers. Jesus had instructed them to wait in Jerusalem until they would be endued with power from on high, (Lu 24:49) but could there be more? Could it also be that God had an eternal purpose in the midst of all their depression, discouragement and unbelief? We are sure He did.

On the night before the crucifixion Jesus warned his disciples that they were about to forsake him. They all swore on their life that it was not going to happen, (Mt 26:31-15) and they were emotionally devastated when it actually did. Peter was told that before the rooster would crow twice he would deny even knowing Jesus three times...and so it was! (Mt 26:69-75, Mk 14:66-72, Lu 22:54-62, Jo 18:15-27) The Bible tells us that immediately after the cock crew he remembered Jesus' prophecy, "and he went out and wept bitterly [that is, with painfully moving grief]." (Lu 22:62, Amp) Now Peter would also have surely remembered Jesus' words: "Whoever denies me before men, him I will deny before My Father." (Mt 10:33) and he was probably thinking he had even lost his salvation, but he should also have remembered Jesus' dying words from the Cross: *It is finished!* (Jn 19:30) The doctrine of the Finished Work [that Christ died for all the sins of all men of all

8

time, once and for all, for all who believe on Him] is crucial as being foundational to our salvation and to understanding divine love. When all else fails—and it will—Love never fails. (1Co 13:8)

They fished all night on the Lake of Tiberias—which they knew like the back of their hand—and caught nothing...more discouragement! Then, very early in the morning someone was calling from the shore, telling them to cast their net on the other side of the boat— actually the shallows, where they would not expect to catch fish, but they did so anyway; they would try anything at this point.

Suddenly...the net was filled with so many fish they could not even pull it into the boat! Now, they knew it was Jesus, and went for the shore pulling their fish-filled nets along with them. Jesus was already roasting fish for breakfast. (Jn 21:9) After they had eaten, Jesus said to Peter, "Simon, son of John, do you truly Love me more than these?" (i.e. more than others do) and "these" must refer to the other Disciples, because that's what Peter meant when he said, "Even if all (these) are made to stumble because of you, I will never be made to stumble." (Mt 26:35) That was when Jesus prophesied: "Assuredly, I say to you that this night, before the rooster crows, you will deny me three times."

Jesus' question about Peter's love for him is important because it is actually a test of his understanding of Love, and it would bring all of them right back to that very night they denied him. Peter's answer reveals that they do not understand; their love for him was human love only—philos. If this were not so they would never have failed him because Love never fails—Love cannot deny Love. It was not that they did not have a new heart that contained Love, but they were often not able to allow *agape* love to control their flesh, so *philos* love did, and it failed miserably every time.

9

> And though I have the gift of prophecy, and understand
> all mysteries and all knowledge, and though I have all
> faith, so that I could remove mountains, but have not
> Love, I am nothing.

1 Corinthians 13:2

Autonomous human love is *quantitative*; God's love
is *qualitative*. The quantity of "love" for the Lord is never
the question; the quality of it always is because I could
have all human love, like all knowledge, or all faith, and
that love would actually be as nothing if I lack quality
love—*agape*. (1Co 13:1-2) Peter's response to Jesus' question
was, "Yes, Lord, you know that I *love* you [that I have
deep, instinctive, personal affection for you, as for a
close friend]." (Jn 21:15, Amp) which is the precise definition
of *philos* love. Jesus responded, "Feed my sheep." and
immediately repeated the same question, "Do you truly
Love me?" again using *agape*, and again Peter's response
was "...Yes; we've been the best of friends since the day
I met you. Of course I love (*philos*) you!" Again Jesus
said, "Feed my sheep." ...He probably hesitated for a
few moments to let it sink in this time. Then, yet a third
time, he asked, "Peter, do you *love* me?" but this time he
used *philos* himself, and Peter again responded, "Yes,
Lord, you are my very best friend; you know that I love
[*philos*] you!" but he was deeply hurt because Jesus
asked him the third time. (Jo 21:17) And Jesus repeated for
the third time, "Feed my sheep."

Now if Jesus was trying to comfort Peter's wounded
emotions—which is often taught concerning this text—
this is obviously not the best way to do it because now
he's hurting more than ever. It must be that Jesus has
another motive for this line of questioning.

Note that while he has one question, "Do you love
me?" he used two distinctly different forms of the
word "love" —*agape* and *phileo*—and he had but one
exhortation every time he asked that question: "Feed
my sheep." Now Peter was very well aware of Jesus' Love

for him, even with *agape* love; and he also had plenty of experience with Jesus' willingness to forgive, but he was not really aware of his potential to respond to Jesus' Love with perfected Love. Do you see it? The problem was not Peter's relationship with Jesus it was Peter's relationship with himself—in his wounded emotions— so it was with all the Disciples, and so it often is with you and I.

They were all in the throes of depression, not because of the crucifixion of Jesus, for they knew he had arisen from the dead, but because they had all abandoned him in the hour of his great need for their support, encouragement, and prayer. (Mt 26:38) Depression, which had its source in guilt, was at the root of their decision to quit their call to the Great Commandment, (Jn 13:34) and the Great Commission. (Mt 28:19,20) The fishers of men (Mt 4:19, Mk 1:17) went back to fishing for fish. From Divine perspective the great problem was not that they had abandoned Jesus, it was that they had abandoned their call to be fishers of men. And that decision definitely originated with wounded emotions.

Jesus' use of *phileo* instead of *agape* in his third question to Peter reveals his willingness to accept Peter's *phileo* response. What does this teach us; the great truth that God's first call on our life is about Him loving us, not about us loving Him. (1Jo 4:19) When we understand this, "Feed my sheep" begins to come into focus because feeding the sheep really means Loving the sheep, something we cannot do unless we're freely receiving Love from the Shepherd himself. (Jn 10:14)

Love is food for the hungry—it produces quality emotions, quality thoughts, quality decisions, and quality disciples, because it is quality love. The Finished Work is vital to the work of the ministry. It is quality work—a labor of quality love. (1Th 1:3, He 6:10) I must be absolutely sure of it: My sin—past, present, and future—was dealt with on the Cross. I will never know the infinite difference between *agape* and *phileo,* and I will be forever trying to turn quantity into quality, until I know my sin has been deleted out of existence. As far as God is concerned, that work is finished forever.

You and I are very much like the Disciples: often devastated by the loss of loved ones, tragedies, disappointments, heart breaking circumstances, guilt, and shame. We easily become depressed as we deal with many details of life. We know God loves us but we often refuse to receive Love because inwardly we feel totally unworthy; or we're simply unaware of our options. We have so much remorse because of our sin that we can't bring ourselves to receive anything from anyone—especially Love from God who is Love! When our emotions are wounded they demand a pity-party, but what they actually want is to manipulate us into allowing them to do our thinking. Often we feel sorry for ourselves, give up, quit, and appease them. But this takes us right out of God's plan and purpose—His calling upon our life. Then, like the Disciples, we fish all night and catch nothing but more depression and discouragement; our best efforts to minister seem to be fruitless, we become discouraged and simply give up. No quantity of autonomous, human love can deliver us from this emotional trap, but quality love can, and it will, if we...just let God love us. How do we do that? We refuse to be discouraged by parlous circumstances; when faced by them we default to truth—the Word and the promises of God—we do not faint, we pray; (Lu 18:1) we count it all joy; (Ja 1:2) we put ourselves in the channel of charity; we go to services, we go on outreaches, we listen to Gospel music, we worship and praise Him who Loves us with eternal, perfect Love.

Jesus gives us the remedy for a wounded heart—three times! As though to say, "Once for the Father, once for the Holy Spirit, and once for Yours Truly."

The heart of Heaven speaks through our Savior:

Feed my sheep! Feed my sheep! Feed my sheep! I know you're wounded, but I was wounded for you. I know you can't respond to *agape* with anything but *phileo* at times, but that's alright! All that went to the Cross; your sins have all been paid for. The work is finished; there is therefore now no condemnation. (Ro 8:1) Put your past behind you, get into the channel of charity: divine love, prayer, the Bible, fellowship in the Body, outreach, Missions! This is quality food for your hungry heart! This is what you need and it is also what the sheep need. Feed my sheep! Let me worry about the fish. I'll even do the cooking...I'll feed you—and you'll feed my sheep!

The focus is upon one thing, feeding the sheep *agape* love. God's last word to His Disciples, as the Old Covenant Dispensation of Law is about to become the New Covenant Dispensation of Grace is: "Feed my sheep!"

Quality love produces quality people.

13

1

Rooted And Founded In Love

"Feed my sheep" actually points to a fundamental need of every soul: to love and to be loved unconditionally. Love is "soul food" for every sheep. Love serves, Love feeds the sheep; it is at once the food of the shepherd, and the food the shepherd feeds the sheep. This is what it means to be a servant of God, a channel of charity: receiving His love, being constrained by His love (2Co 5:14) in seeking and saving the lost, (Lu 19:10) and ministering His love to whosoever will freely receive it by grace through faith.

> May Christ through your faith [actually] dwell (settle down, abide, make His permanent home) in your hearts! May you be rooted deep in love and founded securely in love, that you may have the power and be strong to apprehend and grasp with all the saints [God's devoted people, the experience of that love] what is the breadth and length and height and depth [of it]. [That you may really come] to know [practically, through experience for yourselves] the love of Christ, which far surpasses mere knowledge [without experience]; that you may be filled [through all your being] unto all the fullness of God [may have the richest measure of the divine Presence, and become a body wholly filled and flooded with God Himself]!
>
> Ephesians 3:17-19 (Amplified)

To be a channel of charity, it is essential to be rooted deeply and founded securely in His love. Just as a tree needs to be well rooted in order to assimilate water and nutrients from the soil, just as a structure needs a solid foundation in order to weather storms that test its integrity, so the soul needs a rich diet of Love from above. To be rooted in Love means to have one's life firmly planted in the fertile soil of a fruitful ministry, to be hid in Christ (Co 3:2-3) through life in a Spirit filled Body, active in the hearing and application of the Word, and having a global vision for the saving of souls and the making of disciples.

Being rooted in Love we have the strength of Godly convictions, nurtured in the highways and hedges of outreach and missions; this enables us to experience every dimension of His love—the *breadth, length, height* of it, which is the time-space practical application; and the *depth* of it, which is the spiritual application.

There is a picture of a deer on the run from its hunter; (Ps 42:1-7) tired, covered with foaming sweat, panting, and thirsting, it runs to a spring of clear, cold water. It stops and drinks deeply, and its heart is refreshed. So it is with you and I; our enemies pursue us relentlessly, but we run to the clear, cool, spring of water we know—the fellowship of the Body of Christ, the channel of charity that is our wellspring of Love. We drink long and deeply, and our soul is refreshed and quickened, for Love is the strength of our life. (Ps 27:1) The deep calls to the deep; our spirit calls out to the depths of Love, for it is essential to its vitality. This is how we experience Love; this is how we find strength when our faith is tested by the trials and tribulations of daily life.

To be rooted and founded in Love
is to have a soul built upon
the Rock of our Salvation,
and a spirit that thirsts
for Jesus Christ,
Love personified.

1

The Gift Of Tongues

On the day of Pentecost, not many days after Jesus' appearance to his Disciples on the shores of Tiberius, the promised Holy Spirit [Jo 14:16, 26, 15:26, 16:7, Ac 1:5] came to baptize with fire. [Ac 2:1-3] The instant the Disciples believed—whenever that may have been—they were born again [Jn 3:3-7] and received a new heart and a new spirit, [Ez 11:19, 36:26] a literal *agape* reservoir. [Ro 5:5] But now the Holy Spirit will fill them [Ac 2:4]—anoint them, [1Co 3:16] and seal them. [Ep 1:13] Their new heart will become Christ's Throne Room [Ep 3:17]—the seat of divine authority that enables them, and equips them as ambassadors for Christ. [2Co 5:20] This being accomplished, the Dispensation of Law ends, the Dispensation of Grace begins, and the Church is inaugurated. This is actually what baptism by fire relates to: the experience of God's judgment, which in this case is a Dispensational changeover. [A Dispensation is a period of time wherein God deals with His people according to a specific set of guidelines and/or rules (i.e. The Commandments).]

The next scene in the Bible is amazing: Disciples immediately go out to share the Gospel with multitudes of devout Jews who were gathered in Jerusalem from many nations to celebrate Pentecost. And people were amazed that they were hearing, in their own native tongue, what unlearned Galileans were sharing with them as though they were well-educated men who fluently spoke several languages. [Ac 2:5-13] This actually provides us with a clear picture of what the Church is really all about: Feeding the sheep. And we could say, what every Dispensation has ever been about: God loving the world.

"Do you speak in *tongues,* Pastor Ron?" I've been asked this question many times. Oh, yes; I certainly do! Have you ever witnessed to a group of teenagers on an inner-city street corner, or an intellectual student on a college campus? Have you shared the word of grace with a religious person who has never one time let God love him/her? Have you ever tried to convince a prostitute—a person who has an immense problem believing that God (or anyone else) could love her unconditionally— that God really does love her— that He actually sees her as a virgin in Christ? Have you ever shared your Savior's love with an average man, on an average street, in some average city, Nowheresville, Timbuktu, and you don't know one word of the native tongue, and there's no interpreter available?

Yes! I definitely do speak in tongues; it must be so because there is no possible way I could communicate His love to thousands of everyday people I meet in the streets and cities of this world if I do not.

The language of *agape* has never changed; like Jesus himself it's the same yesterday, today, and forever (He 13:8) in every nation on Planet Earth, as it is in Heaven. My testimony is this: Everyone I speak to, wherever I go, picks-up on the language of Love and understands it immediately; not by power, not by might, but by *His* Spirit, (Ze 4:6) just as they did at Pentecost in Jerusalem, in the very first moments of the Grace Dispensation.

Is "tongues" an angelic language? No, it is not! Tongues is an *agape* language, and I'm sure angels would love to speak it, but they cannot, not because they don't love God, but because they cannot love Him as humans can, any more than we can love Him as angels do. Their love for God is of an eternal order because they were created in eternity; our love for God is of a time-space, faith based order. What angels can do is what they do—encourage us and cover us as we do the communicating of *agape* in this present world.

17

And they do this with great enthusiasm, because they desire to participate in any possible way in a work of faith and Love made perfect. Yes, I do have the gift of tongues because I have the gift of His love working in me and through me, being perfected and manifested in every good work (2Co 9:8)...Praise the Lord!

Peter was suddenly moved by the Spirit of God to stand up and preach the Word in a loud voice. (Ac 2:14) Everyone there heard him in his own native tongue, (Ac 2:6-13) and when his message was finished, three thousand newborn souls were ushered into the Kingdom of God. (Ac 2:14-41) What a scene! What an awesome demonstration of the power of Holy Spirit-anointed, perfected Love winning souls to Christ! What awesome power Love has to encourage us in the faith, to motivate hearts in the Great Commission to win the lost, to baptize, to make disciples, and to teach what Jesus taught—The Great Commandment:

Let God love you!
Then you will Love God,
then you will Love yourself;
then you will Love others;
then you will Love
...even your enemies.

1

Love's Virtues

> And though I have the gift of prophecy, and understand all mysteries and all knowledge, and though I have all faith, so that I could remove mountains, but have not love, I am nothing.
>
> 1 Corinthians 13:2

If I understood all mysteries and had all knowledge, I would be a great prophet indeed, but this is not possible. The Bible assures me that if I had all faith I could actually move mountains, (Mt 21:21) and I would be a renowned, mountain-moving Christian, but this isn't possible either. These statements are hyperboles: not to be understood in a literal sense; exaggerated. But let us assume for a moment that they actually are possible; then the greatest, mountain-moving prophet of all time would be God, and even all of His knowledge, and understanding, and wonderful works would have no value whatsoever if He had not Love. I could be all things to all men, and still be nothing, without Love as the basis of all my works.

It's interesting to consider the opposite aspect of a hyperbole. If we do, then what might seem to be the simplest prophecy, or the smallest act of faith, by the least of God's servants, if their works actually do have their motive in Love, then they truly do have great potential to be fruitful because they glorify God in the very essence of His nature, which is Love. But that's not all; now Love has taken a step beyond human knowledge by manifesting itself through human weakness. (Ep 3:19) This is truly amazing grace!

And though I bestow all my goods to feed the poor, and though I give my body to be burned, but have not love, it profits me nothing.

Verse 3

I could be the kindest, most generous, compassionate person on Planet Earth, yet all my good deeds would profit me absolutely nothing if they were not accomplished by Love working *in* me and *through* me. Many noble people are very generous in giving of themselves and their resources to many a great and good cause, and we are very thankful that they do, but in eternal terms the net value of all their works is absolute zero if they were not constrained by Love in every good work they performed. (2Co 5:14) I could add-up my entire life, every good thing I've ever done, every good thing about me— my good looks + my good nature + my generosity + my good reputation + my good words + my hard work + my tithes + my offerings + my donations + all the times I went to Church + all the hours I spent on my knees in prayer, worshipping God, praising Jesus, etc., etc., etc., and the sum total of it all = one big, fat ZERO ...if I have not Love.

Pr. Tom Schaller:

The memory of a Buddhist, monk who actually did give his body to be burned in protest of the Vietnam War back in the 60's, is very vivid in my mind. He sat down in the midst of a public square, in full view of television cameras, and doused himself with high-octane gasoline, and ignited it with a match. His life in this world ended right then and there, but the war did not; it went on for years, and wars and rumors of wars abound to this day. (Mt 24:6, Mk 13:7, Lu 21:9) I could even argue that the monk's sacrifice of himself might have had at least some impact upon the war, but the real question is this: Did he have Love? Was this a demonstration of God's love working through him, or was it not? Because, if not, the burning of his body profited him nothing! In all truth, his body burns yet again in hell—forever...where the worm does not die and the fire is not quenched, (Mk 9:44,46,48) if he never did receive the Love that paid for His sin on the Cross.

> Love suffers long and is kind,
>
> Verse 4a

How long is "long"? It could be a very, very long time! The original language interprets "long" from the Greek, meaning to be long-spirited, or patient; and the root word means to be lenient, willing to lower the standard when it comes to discipline. "Long" means as long as it takes to accomplish what grace always does: manifest Love until its work is finished.

Sometimes I need grace; (Ro 5:2) sometimes I need great grace; (Ac 4:33) and sometimes I need grace for grace. (Jo 1:16) I need grace to deal with every detail of life; I need great grace when I'm called of God to a great work, and I need grace for grace to deal with special areas of my life that only God fully understands (i.e. being a teenager, or elderly, or blind from birth). Grace is always there, because Love is always there, and Love always gives itself to meet our need; (He 4:16) it gives leniently, patiently, and is kind throughout the entire process.

I may be going through a very difficult time. It may be that I lost my job, I lost my wife, I lost my all my friends, I lost my health, I lost my fame and fortune, I lost my home, or all the above (God forbid it); but now I feel that I just need to go to a barroom, drown my woes in alcohol, choke them with cigarette smoke...But, NO! Love suffers long! Love is kind! Love does not hurt Love; especially God who is Love. So I love God; I Love my wife; I Love my Pastor; I Love the Body; I love soul winning because I Love the lost; I Love myself; I Love those who don't Love me one iota. And if I really do Love I will really take great care to always honor Love with long suffering and kindness.

...Love does not envy,

Verse 4b

Love harbors no feelings of discontent, or resentment aroused by the possessions, or qualities, or blessings of others; contrariwise, it actually rejoices in them.

...Love does not parade itself, is not puffed up,

Verse 4c

Love is not boastful or vainglorious; it is ever careful not to show excessive pride or self-satisfaction in its achievements, possessions, or abilities. It never displays itself in an arrogant or disdainful way, because it is not inflated with pride and conceit.

... [Love] does not behave rudely,

Verse 5a

Love does not act in a rude, or an un-gentlemanly, or un-ladylike, or any other improper manner; it's not disgraceful, indecent, degrading, dishonorable, undignified or indiscreet in any way whatsoever.

... [Love] does not seek its own,

Verse 5b

Love doesn't insist on having its own way, or its rights; it is not egotistical, egocentric, self-seeking, self-serving, self-absorbed, self-obsessed, self-interested, or self-anything.

... [Love] is not provoked,

Verse 5c

Love is not touchy, fretful, and irritable, stressed, uptight, bad-tempered, grumpy, crabby, or crotchety; nor is it indignant, put out, dissatisfied, disgruntled, better, miffed, peeved, or sore.

Love suffers...
for as long as necessary
and it is kind
throughout the entire process.

1

Evil Thinking

Love suffers long, and is kind; love does not envy; love does not parade itself, is not puffed up, does not behave rudely, seeks not its own, is not provoked, thinks no evil...

1 Corinthians 13:4-5

Thinking evil probably gets us into more trouble than any other sin. Evil spirits have an innate ability to project evil thoughts. When we entertain these projections our own thoughts are but one small step away from becoming evil actions. But Love casts down every evil thought that sets itself up against true knowledge of God, and leads every thought away captive to the obedience of Christ. [1Co 10:5] True knowledge of God is ever conscious of His love, that His thoughts toward us are always good—never evil—to give us hope and a future. [Je 29:11]

Love takes no account of any evil thing it has suffered; it thinks nothing at all of any wrong that has been done it. But when charity *isn't* thinking, evil *is* thinking, and it's only a matter of time before it causes trouble. Conversely, Love thoughts cover a multitude of sin. [1Pe 4:8]

Charles Finney:

Thinking evil [is]...forming unjust opinions of others, and giving indulgence to feelings in correspondence with our unjust opinions...so is thinking enviously.

If I'm envious of anyone—and of course at times I am—I'm thinking evil in my heart. But I confess, "Lord, this is my evil heart thinking." and I purposely turn my thoughts to the Cross where I see my sin crucified with Christ, [Ga 2:20] I see myself crucified in Him, dead, buried, and resurrected; [Ro 6:4-6] yes, even ascended, and seated above in Heavenly places in Him. [Ep 2:6] I consider and sometimes pause to meditate upon each step of this awesome process of grace, and mercy, and Love. By the time I get to the last step I can't even remember what I was thinking about before I started. Then I just thank God for His forgiveness, pray for a fresh filling of the Holy Spirit, and instantly Love is shed abroad in my heart and evil thinking flees from me. Dealing with evil thinking in my life is just that simple.

"Suspicious" thinking is a very common form of evil thinking. To be suspicious is to distrust someone, to have the idea or impression that someone is dishonest, not trustworthy, of questionable character, dangerous, or involved in something dishonest or illegal. And I ask myself if I'm ever suspicious of anyone? A brother? A sister? A friend? Someone I don't even know personally? A passer-by? A co-worker? A Pastor? Yes, of course I am; who isn't? But I do not have to allow my thoughts to be suspicious. I can choose to be governed by the nature of Love. When I do, my mind sees everything and everyone in a totally different frame of reference—one that is rooted and founded in the nature of God, who is Love [1Jn 4:8,16] and never thinks evil. Now my suspicions are cast down with every other thing that exalts itself against a true knowledge of God; this is how I take my suspicious thinking captive into the obedience of Christ in me, where it is crucified—dead.

Pr. Tom Schaller:

Is God ever aware of evil thinking in us? Yes! Jesus was very well aware of evil thinking in the heart of Judas Iscariot. He knew Satan was standing at his right hand, [Ps 109:6] he knew he would betray him

25

with a kiss when the Temple guard came to arrest him in the Garden of Gethsemane, (Lu 22:48) and he also knew Judas was a money-grabbing thief—yet he allowed him to manage the moneybag. (Jo 13:29) He knew Judas had serious problems, that in his heart he was not with the rest of them, but Jesus framed him in his every thought without any evil whatsoever and actually referred to him and loved him as his friend. (Mt 26:50) Was Jesus ever suspicious of Judas? No, he was not! He had discernment concerning him; he was not naive, he knew who Judas was—that he was not one of the twelve—but his mind was never for one instant suspicious. Love does not think that way; Love's nature is always altruistic.

The old adage is: "Set a rouge to catch a rogue". One who has a heart that has not Love has made suspicion an art form, and knows all the ways and means of suspicion; he is a suspicious rogue. If he's a hypocrite, he will suspect others of being hypocritical, because he's very familiar with that frame of mind; if he's a liar, or a thief, or a murderer, he'll suspect everyone he meets to be one also. Contrariwise, the heart of love is so conscious of its own righteousness in Christ that it is totally unable to see anyone else any other way.

Evil thinking dwells upon the faults of others (real or imaginary), even when it's unwarranted to do so:

Charles Finney:

I know a man who always finds fault with his wife. He never notices her many, excellent qualities; his mind feeds upon her faults continually, and when he speaks of her, only faultfinding comes out. Even though his heart truly loves her, his mind is so totally saturated with her faults that it cannot express love. It may be that he's not saved, and has not charity; or it may be that he is saved, but charity is stifled in him, because it has no charitable frame of reference in the Word of God. If a husband would actually love his wife as Christ loved the church, (Ep 5:25) his heart would be grieved at the slightest hint of a fault in her, and his mouth would be unable to speak of it because his mind would not even recognize what it is.

Evil thinking also dwells upon personal injuries (real or imaginary) received from others. It's very easy for me to carry a grudge or a chip-on-my-shoulder when I've been hurt by someone, even if I only think I have. This kind of thinking is altogether void of charity, and actually has its roots firmly established in *iniquity*. Iniquity operates from the frame of reference of wounded emotions to control the mental process whereby the emotions do the thinking; it usurps every authority of the government of the soul. This thinking is not coordinated with the charitable, new heart; this is thinking energized by the old heart which is desperately wicked, deceitful above all things, (Je 17:9) and definitely does not have Love.

> ...[Love] does not rejoice in iniquity, but rejoices in the truth; bears all things, believes all things, hopes all things, endures all things.
>
> Verse 6-7

Pr. Tom Schaller:

As I often travel abroad I can't help but wonder at the Love we share for one another on our foreign mission fields. It would be very easy to allow differences to drive us apart because there are many; cultural, social, economic, and political, just to mention a few. We often minister to people who are immensely underprivileged compared to ourselves, and we might imagine that they feel we're obliged to help them in their poverty. Some actually do feel that way and they're bitter or resentful when we do not help them.

Others may wonder: Is your teaching correct? Can we really believe what you tell us? Can we trust you? What are your real motives?

It's easy for these thoughts to dominate the minds of those we minister to, there's no question about it, but my testimony is this: If we have real love in our hearts, it will always cast the most positive light possible over all our meetings. This is where we have true fellowship, and it's because there is no evil thinking whatsoever. We believe that we are Loved even if our email didn't get answered; that we really are cared for, even though we never did get a visit at our home. We're not meeting one another with suspicion we're meeting one another with Love. And it doesn't matter one iota what color our skin is, or how many possessions we have, or don't have. We couldn't possibly care less if someone is intelligent or ignorant, young or old, rich or poor. We Love one another as Jesus Christ loves us, because His love is in us, His love thinks with His mind, and we really do have his mind. (1Co 2:16) We Love, we trust, and we care because we're constrained by Love shed abroad in our hearts by the Holy Spirit. (2Co 5:14, Ro 5:5) Love thinks no evil. We may have done very little for one another—if anything at all—but we discern that much actually has been done in Christ simply because God loves us, we Love God, we Love one another, and we even Love our enemies. Whatever we do, regardless of how much or how little, we know it's all a labor of Love. (He 6:10)

There were many from Turkey at our European conference in Budapest, Hungary, and they were very thankful to God to be in our presence. They would often say to our missionaries:

Why did you come to Turkey?

You didn't have to come here...but you did! Why?

Did you study your Bible? Was it for your sake, or just for our sake?

Why do you say prayers for the people of Turkey?

Why not other people?

Why do you invest your time, and your money, and your life, and many other resources in Turkey, of all places? Why?

It must be that there is Love in you; it must be so, because we know that this is precisely what Love always does. Only Love could ever have this kind of compassion on us.

Charles Finney:

A charitable mind thinketh no evil. This is plain and very true. It is not however implied that charitable men are blind to facts, or that they are incapable of thinking of things as they are.

Our Love for one another is the real thing; it's not phony, it's not a put-on, we're not naive to the facts of life, and we absolutely do know what's going on in this world. We know there's a Judas Iscariot out there, we know there are problems here and there...we know, but we also know God is sovereign, omniscient, that He sees things—even evil things—with divine perspective. He has the big picture—past, present, and future—and He esteems it all in His real nature, and controls it with perfect love, which is very real...that's *agape*! T h e mind of the spiritual man is under the control of Love. When we have Love working in us, we're able to conduct ourselves in faith; when things aren't exactly right Love is there, we're Loving, long suffering, kind, not enviable, not proud, not puffed-up, not misbehaving, not seeking our own, not easily provoked, bearing all things, believing all things, hoping all things, and enduring all things without ever allowing our mind to think evil.

As an illustration let's say I'm happily driving down the Interstate one day and I suddenly have a flat tire. Immediately I say, or I think, "Ah! Darn it!" [Or something much worse.] "Why do things like this always happen to me? Do I need this? I wonder what idiot dropped that nail—or whatever it was—right on the highway?"

And what is this but casting over my situation a way of thinking which is derived, not from my *new* heart, but from my *evil,* old heart—my sin nature. My mind is actively entertaining evil; Love has nothing at all to do with it. But let's put the situation in the light of a charitable mind. How do I see myself in the situation now? I understand that God is in every millisecond of every single detail of my life, every square millimeter, every thought, and every impulse of my brain. He knew exactly where my tire was, and indubitably where the nail (or whatever) was at precisely the moment they came into contact. He knew where I was, how I would react, He was in control of the steering wheel, doing what God does in me according to His perfect plan and purpose, every infinitesimal instant of my life. He foreordained every detail of this incident with the intention of blessing me—Jeremiah 29:11.

Praise God for his goodness! Let everything that has breath; praise ye the Lord! Praise the Lord—Psalm 150:6. All things work together for good to those that love God—Romans 8:28. I will bless the Lord at all times; His praise shall continually be in my mouth—Psalm 34:1. In everything give thanks, for this is the will of God in Christ Jesus for you—1 Thessalonians 5:18. Now I can say, "Thank you, Jesus, for this fabulous, flat tire. Praise You, Lord! I Praise You, Lord! Praise you! Thank you, Lord...and please help me to fix it with joy in my heart. Amen!"

Now, which mind is thinking evil, and which mind is thinking charitable? That's easy! Love thinks no evil.

Pr. Tom Schaller:

At our conference in Europe, we were dripping with the oil of the presence of the Lord, and the manifestation of Love in the Body of Christ. The anointing with every message was one of precision and clarity. Hearts were touched and some precious people were in tears, all the way to the back row of the auditorium. All of us were caught up in the spirit of Love, and even though the service was over, couldn't leave the room for hours just for the joy of pure fellowship. We were continually shaking hands, greeting and hugging one another, and praising God for his goodness, mercy, and Love.

I must say, there could have been many reasons for dissention and division, but Love has enormous power in the lives of God's people to release amazing miracles of healing and deliverance. Love has awesome potential to turn a curse from the pit of hell itself into a blessing from Heaven. We were all a witness to the power of perfected Love; into the night, and even the following day, we were rejoicing—not in iniquity, but rejoicing in the truth.

> Love never fails. But whether there are prophecies, they will fail; whether there are tongues, they will cease; whether there is knowledge, it will vanish away.
>
> Verse 8

There is absolutely no substitute for Love. Be it prophecy, or tongues, or knowledge, or any other form we might imagine love to take, no matter how sincere, or romantic, or religious, or intense it may be...it shall vanish away.

Let Love do its work,
and evil thinking will FLEE!

31

1

Victory Because Of Love

There is no fear in love; but perfect love casts out fear, because fear involves torment. But he who fears has not been made perfect in love.

1 John 4:18

We have no idea how fragile, and yet how powerful, we are...because of Love. God's Word tells us that we're fearfully and wonderfully made. (Ps 139:14) If we take wonderfully to mean that, in our humanity, we have a wonderful potential to glorify our Creator as we respond to Love, this must be His primary purpose in all of creation. Then "fearfully" means that we're pathetically vulnerable to being fearful whenever we're estranged from Love.

The destruction of our relationship with God is a primary cause of the devil in his quest to dishonor God and bring about our demise in the process.

But thanks be to God, who gives us the victory through our Lord Jesus Christ.

1 Corinthians 15:57

One way or another, most of our cares and woes in this world are rooted in fear, because of failed love. The dictionary defines fear as: "An unpleasant emotion caused by the belief that someone or something is dangerous, likely to cause pain, or be a threat to one's safety." And we could add, "...because of a lack of unfailing love."

From the moment of conception we have an intrinsic need in the very depths of our soul for the security of an unfailing love. God created us for Love, His love, to receive it from Him, and to share it with others; (Jo 13:34, 15:9-12) this is our design from the beginning. But the sin of Adam and Eve left them, and all they would produce, with an un-natural fear of God, which is born of guilt and shame; these fears torment us, and leave us totally unable to receive Love until we receive Jesus Christ as Savior.

I have a testimony relating to a memory that takes me back to a time when I was still a babe in my mother's arms—probably only a few months after birth: It must have been in January or February of 1935, just a few months after I was born. Of course I wasn't yet walking, so my mother was carrying me in her arms as she walked from our house to Grandma's, about a half mile down an old, unpaved, country road. I don't know the details as to why the trip was necessary, but they must have been important, because it was during a terrible, New England blizzard, and we would not have been out otherwise. Being born early in December, my approximate age must have been only 2-3 months. I remember looking out over my mother's shoulder through the folds of a warm blanket that had most of my face covered. I was looking at an old barn with an attached stonewall, and a huge tree, when suddenly a strong gust of icy, cold wind whistled and swirled up around us; the blanket was blown back, and uncovered my head, everything went white for a few moments. It only startled me at first; then I was frightened! I was trying to scream but snow showered my face, and took my breath away! Then as suddenly as it began, there was a calm; the wind stopped, it was over and everything was OK—I screamed anyway just to make sure!

I can still see that blowing, swirling snow! I can still hear the whistling of the wind, and feel the icy bite of cold snow on my face! I can see every detail as clearly as though it happened yesterday. And I hate the cold wind to this day! I can't remember any other thing that far back in my life, and 75 years later I can't remember where the toilet is on a given day, but I definitely have not forgotten one detail of this moment in time!

A seemingly insignificant incident, but as an infant, this experience was so intense that the memory of it was indelibly burned into the consciousness of my mind. Ordinarily we're not able to remember things that happen at such an early age, but fear has that kind of power. Often deep wounds are swept under the carpet of the subconscious, only to surface when energized by familiar circumstances; then they cause much emotional turmoil in our life, and we have no clue as to what ever really set them off.

> Perfect love casts out fear, because fear involves torment.
> But he who fears has not been made perfect in love.

1 John 4:18

Having not been made perfect in Love a person is actually unsaved, and the heart is void of divine love; not that God does not Love the sinner, but if the sinner has never received Christ, he/she has effectually never really received God's love; therefore, the power of fear has free course to usurp authority over the heart and cause negative reactions. This may also be the case with a believer if he has received Love but refuses to allow it to rule his life. And it may be a small incident, but when it settles in the subconscious frame of reference of the mind it may become a monstrous phobia—a morbid fear of certain situations, or circumstances, or even people. Others may be astonished that so small a thing could cause such a huge reaction, but truth-be-known, the influence of fear is anything but small in the mind of one who has internalized it.

Demonic forces often target children and young people because it is much easier to establish strongholds of fear in a soul-structure when it has not yet had time to become rooted and grounded in God's love.

The great tragedy of original sin is that it severed us from divine love, leaving us at the mercy of human love. Autonomous human love inevitably fails, and we don't even like to think about the pain and insecurity we experience when it does. When love fails—even one time—it is sure to leave us with an element of fear. If it failed once, sooner or later, it will fail again. Those of us who believe, have received, and are complete in His love; (Co 2:10) thankful forever, knowing that nothing can ever again separate us from Love. (Ro 8:38-39)

We have an innate need to be loved and to love others; yet we fear love, because, often enough, the only love we know—human love—we also know to be fragile and vulnerable to breakdown. It is no wonder that marriages fail, that homosexuality and lesbianism are an acceptable lifestyle, that pornography is readily available—even to children. We could go on, and on, with one grievous testimony after another about the failure of human love, and our desperation to somehow meet our need for love without destroying our life—or someone else's life—in the process. People need love; people need to love others, and many are desperate enough to try anything in order to have that need fulfilled, even if it means un-natural love, even if it is at the expense of someone else—a loving wife, or an innocent child.

Sometimes we can handle it for a while, and even keep a positive attitude while we do—we humans are very skillful at putting up a good front—but sometimes we simply cannot. Sometimes fear haunts our heart continuously until the subconscious mind envelops the bad memory that caused it; now the mind will not allow us to think about it any more. But it's still present with us, deeply imbedded at a subconscious level of the emotional frame of reference, and it is very real. At this point fear has been internalized—it is a very real part of our identity—and actually caused a deformation of the soul-structure. A stronghold has been established and we're not even aware of it; others may be when we react in an adverse way, but we say, "This is just who I am; God made me this way." Is this true? Yes and no; it is who they are and that's the problem, but God had nothing to do with it because God is love, and Love thinks no evil. God's thoughts toward us are always good, never evil, to give us hope and a future. (Je 29:11)

I've known people—and counseled many—who are absolutely convinced that they're born losers. They're not! God never created a loser! This mindset is a direct result of human love trying to live up to the standard of perfect love, failing over, and over, and over again. This is fertile ground for projections from the pit of hell—the seeds of strongholds.

In certain situations deformations of the soul's frame of reference, hidden in the subconscious mind, surface to radically affect thinking. Evil spirits have the ability to access these deformations and they know precisely how, when, and where to use them as strongholds in spiritual warfare, (2Co 10:4) because they have knowledge of us that reaches back into our very genetics. So they project lies, half-truths, deception, suspicion, and evil thinking of all sorts from one stronghold to another, from one person to another, from one situation to another; always with one objective: to stimulate and encourage emotions to usurp authority over decision-making. Why? Because wounded emotions can be very deceptive and ruthless as they maneuver to protect themselves from further pain and injury and/or the agony of unfulfilled, intrinsic needs:

"Why did your mother allow this to happen? Where was Father? Where was God?"

"Does your "Heavenly Father" love and protect His children? Yes, of course He does, but you're so bad you're probably not even saved, let alone be His child.

"It works for others, but it just doesn't work for you, does it?"

"If God doesn't love you, why do you imagine that *anyone* ever will?"

"You need to be way more careful about who you trust; like, maybe they [other parts of this mental process of ours; i.e. mind, volition, conscience, self consciousness] should listen to *me* once in awhile. After all, who always gets hurt when they're wrong? Hmmm? Where this "love" business is concerned, I'm the only one qualified to do the thinking cause it's always me that gets hurt!"

"All you need is a different wife/husband; someone who really knows how to love you. Then life will be a bowl of cherries."

"God made me this way; doesn't the Bible say that some place? So how bad can it be if I'm gay? I'm just being who God made me to be!"

"God knows it: I have this need and if it's not fulfilled those who love me won't be happy either; if its only for their sake, I must do what I must do; they will understand."

This is classic, subjective thinking energized from a demonic stronghold. Why is this strategy exciting to demons? Because they know our emotions are not designed to think; they're design is to respond, not to dictate response. When wounded emotions take over the heart—the attitude of the government of the soul—it's always from a premise of pure self-preservation. Evil and unclean spirits systematically use this process to stir up hatred, strife, and evil thinking in relationships, in churches, in marriages, in friendships, in business, in schools, in governments, in religions, in nations, in cultures, and in every discipline of life. Every relationship, every institution, every individual without God's love as its foundation is a target-of-opportunity for principalities, powers, rulers of the darkness of this world, and spiritual wickedness in high places. (Ep 6:12)

Humanity's history is soaked
with blood,
sweat,
and tears,
as it seeks a solution to its great dilemma—lost
Love—
for it seeks a solution
apart from God who IS love.

1

Strongholds Demolished

Jesus was teaching in a local synagogue on the Sabbath and there was a woman present who had a spirit of infirmity eighteen years. "Infirmity" is translated from the original Greek, *astheneia*: a psychological disorder, i.e. a psychosomatic illness. She was bowed over; in no way could she straighten herself up. (Lu 13:11) She had an ailment energized by a spirit. Her wounded soul had become a veritable prison of guilt and fear that caused a physical ailment, and the devil had the key to it. Satan himself, the prince of evil spirits, had bound her (Lu 13:16) ...with a stronghold. And she was bowed over as though her entire body was burdened with shame because of some terrible sin. I would think she would be desperate to get to Jesus for healing, but she—like so many of us—felt that she just was not worthy. Eighteen years ago—possibly in early childhood—she was terribly abused and emotionally wounded. And the guilt and fear experienced in that incident became internalized: It was her identity; she was her sin! Horror of horrors! Try to imagine it! Then let's think of ourselves; how often we fall prey to the devil's lies about who we really are. Is it any wonder that we are insecure?

When Jesus saw this poor, broken woman, he called her to him and she came—of course she did—but she could not look up to see his face, even if she wanted to. She was helpless before her adversary. Hopelessly resigned to her condition, all she could really do is...let God love her. And that's all she did.

Jesus said, "Woman, you are loosed from your infirmity!" and he laid his hands on her. She was probably looking at his feet when she felt that gentle

39

touch of His love. It emanated from Him, it began to saturate her entire being; she could feel the warmth of it surging through her entire being...and her body was straightened! And Satan was repulsed—he silently and instantly fled from the scene. If we were there we would be absolutely astonished by the power of pure, perfect love. After eighteen years of hell on earth this precious soul stood up, looked into the eyes of Perfect Love, and glorified God. (Lu 13:12,13)   This must be on a parallel with what it will be like for us to see him face to face. (1Co 13:12) Oh; how wonderful it will be when I can stand up straight; totally free from this body of sin and death and look into the eyes of my Savior—my King—face to face. We have a tremendous victory—over Satan himself —because of Love.

> But you are a shield around me, O Lord; you bestow glory on me and lift up my head.
>
> Psalm 3:2 (NIV)

In the face of all logic, reason, argument, theory, or anything contrary to a true knowledge of God, submit to Love...

> For though we walk (live) in the flesh, we are not carrying on our warfare according to the flesh and using mere human weapons. For the weapons of our warfare are not physical [weapons of flesh and blood], but they are mighty before God for the overthrow and destruction of strongholds. [Inasmuch as we] refute arguments and theories and reasoning and every proud and lofty thing that sets itself up against the true knowledge of God; and we lead every thought and purpose away captive into the obedience of Christ.
>
> 2 Corinthians 10:3-4 (Amplified)

When fear is present, the only effective weapon against it is not physical, or chemical, or psychological, or philosophical...it's spiritual. The warfare is on a spiritual plane, and our weapon is spiritual, and it's mighty before God, because, in all truth, it is truth, and it is God—Love, in person...

Our flesh will try to preserve itself by encouraging wounded emotions to dominate the thought process with human reasoning, which invariably will produce false knowledge of God, and set itself up to defend strongholds. Conversely, true knowledge of God always reveals His love for us. (Je 31:3, Jn 3:16, Ep 2:4-5) We disprove every contradiction to truth and every form of false knowledge of Him when, by faith, we simply receive His love—because we actually receive Him when we do. Then he takes his rightful place on the throne of our heart, and the mind of Christ breaks through; (1Co 2:16) emotions are flooded with peace like a river (Is 66:12) and strongholds are demolished—cast into the deepest part of the sea, (Mi 7:19) removed from us as far as the east is from the west (Ps 103:12)—sent into Nothingness, a place where even Omniscience cannot remember sins.

The obedience of Christ
always gives us the victory...
because of Love.

41

1

Love: The Key To Victory

And now abide faith, hope, love, these three; but the greatest of these is love.

1 Corinthians 13:13

Many times in the Bible we find people whose health was pathetic. They lived in an age when there was precious little that could be done for them. Multitudes relied upon superstition, old wives tales, and legends for healing of all kinds of serious ailments, many of which were very painful and totally incurable.

The Pool at Bethesda, by the Sheep Gate of Jerusalem, had five porches around it. Periodically a mysterious angel would stir its waters. The legend was, if one could be the first into the pool when it was stirred, he would be healed of whatever ailment he had. And thousands of people with diverse diseases and afflictions waited for days, weeks, and even years in the shelter of these porches, hoping for healing. A certain crippled man lay there on a pallet waiting for thirty-eight years. (Jn 5:5) Then one day Jesus passed by and saw him, and knew he had suffered for many years. Moved with compassion he asked him, Do you really want to he healed. The man answered, "Yes!! Of course I do! But I have nobody to help me into the water; and when I try to help myself someone always gets there ahead of me." (Jn 5:7)

Of course he would say that! But why would Jesus ask this question in the first place, if he already knew the man had been there for so long? Only because He wants you and I to know what a pitifully, hopeless case this poor

42

man really was. And he almost certainly had acquired his infirmity via some personal sin, because later in the context of this same chapter we find that Jesus met him in the Temple, and warned him saying, Sin no more lest a worse thing come upon you. (Jn 5:14) If we knew the man we would probably be thinking that He deserved to suffer, that God was punishing him for some evil sin. He was absolutely unable to help himself, and nobody was about to help him because he was cursed of God. But Jesus said, "Rise, take up your bed and walk. And immediately the man was made well, took up his bed, and walked. (Jn 5:8-9) The Lord Jesus Christ met him right where he was, not with indifference or condemnation, but with love. No one knows how the man recognized Love, but somehow he did, and he will remember it forever. Without faith it is impossible to please God; without hope we will be miserable failures indeed; *faith* and *hope* are precious time-space commodities, but *Love is eternal.*

C. H. Spurgeon:

Men do not make themselves love by a course of calculation; but they are overtaken with it, and carried away by its power. When godly men consider and enjoy the great love of God to them, they begin to love God in return; just as the bud, when it feels the sunshine, opens to it of its own accord. Love to God is a sort of natural consequence, which follows from a sight and sense of the love of God to us. I think it is Aristotle who says that it is impossible for a person to know that he is loved without feeling some degree of love in return. I do not know how that may be, for I am no philosopher; but I am sure that it is so with those who taste of the love of God. As love is the first blessing coming from God to us, so it is the last return from us to God; he comes to us loving...we go home to him loving.

If I were to try to open a rosebud by my own hand, I would surely destroy it, but as soon as the sun shines upon it, it begins to open. And I could never Love in my strength alone but His love in me is its own source. So it is with God's love; there is no substitute for its power. Many waters (i.e. a gigantic *tsunami*) cannot quench love. (SS 8:7) The presence of love cannot be over-looked any more than the very presence of God can be overlooked. At Bethesda it energized the compassion of Christ, it radiated from him, and immediately the man was made whole. After thirty-eight miserable years of failure and rejection he got the victory...because of love.

A woman with an issue of blood for twelve years tried everything, and everyone, but there was no healing for her until Jesus passed by. The Bible tells us that she pushed her way through a huge crowd, lunged at him, and managed to just touch the very tip of the hem of His garment—not even his person—and she was instantly healed when virtue surged out of Him (Lu 8:44) *Virtue?* Yes! Power! (Greek: *dunamis*) The Amplified Bible translates virtue: healing power.

All who experience the healing power
latent in Love
are changed forever.

Pr. Tom Schaller:

All through my years of ministry I've been ever thankful for the Body of Christ and every faithful servant of God. They did not have to study the Bible, but they did; they did not have to minister to me, and put their hands on my shoulder and say, You're going to make it, but they did; people did not have to pray for us, but they did, and the result is that this ministry is now sending missionaries into all the world with the Gospel. It all came from hearts that were filled with *agape* love. *Agape* is the most powerful thing in the life of all who believe.

Let's be thankful and prayerful, praising God at all times and in every place; let's keep ourselves in the love of God, (Ju 21) and let's keep ourselves from thinking evil, (1Co 13:5) and from putting evil upon everything and everyone—even ourselves. Don't ever think about yourself that way; always see yourself in the context of God's love. Oh! How much better it is to just let God love us, because He really, really, really does! He loves us! He loves us! He loves us! He loves us with everlasting, unconditional, *agape* love, and we love Him; not just in our emotions, but in a way that absolutely thinks with God.

We're sure to have many disappointments in this life. (Ps 34:19; Jn 14:1) And we're sure to have trials and tribulations in this world, but Jesus overcame the world, (Jo 16:33) and so will we because Love will give us the victory. The promise is: He will always cause us to triumph, (2Co 2:14) we will always be victorious, (1Co 15:57) and we're always more than conquerors through Him who loves us, (Ro 8:37) because Love never fails.

Pr. Tom Schaller:

In our church we have a little, 83-year-old lady who is from Turkmenistan. I call her our "Greater Grace Mother Theresa" because she actually does look much like her. What is more, she has that same heart of love. And she's very durable for her age. A few years ago she got hit by a car, and had to go to the hospital, but she wasn't injured at all. Actually, the car probably suffered more damage than she did!

When she was serving with our ministry in Turkey, she went to the Pastor one day and said, 'I like to work; is there something I can do?' He told her she could clean up a few of the chairs in the church if she wanted to, and was able—not really believing she was. But that little lady cleaned and polished forty-five chairs; for two days she polished away until every one of them sparkled like new.

Whenever I see her I say to myself, "There it is! That's it! That's the new heart He gives us! (Ez 36:26) That's the love He gives us! That's what we have! We have what she has! Yes!! We have it too, because that's how we think. That's how we live! That's how we endure! That's how we believe! That's how we love one another! That's how we touch the world, the love of Christ working in us and through us! That's perfected Love!"

We have great power to accomplish amazing things— i.e. put men on the moon—but if we don't have Love, whatever is done actually means nothing at all to God, and it's only a matter of time before we see its utter failure, because it's twisted and distorted, and wrong. We may have faith that can move mountains, but its actually sin, not faith at all, if it's not faith that works by Love, but if it *is* ...O my! What awesome power perfected Love has to always give us the victory. (1Jn 5:4)

We check our heart many times over every day to be sure we're living in the love of God. We cannot afford to think outside of it, not for an instant. We let God love us, and search our hearts, and our minds, and say: "Yes!! We want to live like God, and love like God in this world! We want to be victorious because of Love."

Love is eminently patient and kind in its suffering; humble in its heart, mannerly, without envy, selfless, easygoing, unsuspicious, and never finds fault with others, because it is forever conscious of its victory in the love of Jesus Christ.

> What shall we say of these things? And what shall we do?
>
> Romans 8:31

Pr. Tom Schaller:

We shall pray that God will continually fill us with the Spirit of Love. Then we will be equipped to bear all things, believe all things, hope all things, and endure all things, because Love never fails! Love always wins! Our Lord Jesus Christ died with Love in his heart. He was the greatest winner of all time, and so are we!

What shall say to these things? We shall say, "We have the victory because of Love!" And we shall pray that God will fill us with the Spirit of Love.

Chapter 2
— Objective Love —

Water Turned Into Wine

On the third day there was a wedding in Cana of Galilee, and the mother of Jesus was there. Now both Jesus and His disciples were invited to the wedding. And when they ran out of wine, the mother of Jesus said to Him, "They have no wine." Jesus said to her, "Woman, what does your concern have to do with me? My hour has not yet come." His mother said to the servants, "Whatever He says to you, do it." Now there were set there six water pots of stone, according to the manner of purification of the Jews, containing twenty or thirty gallons apiece. Jesus said to them, "Fill the water pots with water." And they filled them up to the brim. And He said to them, "Draw some out now, and take it to the master of the feast." And they took it. When the master of the feast had tasted the water that was made wine, and did not know where it came from (but the servants who had drawn the water knew), the master of the feast called the bridegroom. And he said to him, "Every man at the beginning sets out the good wine, and when the guests have well drunk, then the inferior. You have kept the good wine until now!" This beginning of signs Jesus did in Cana of Galilee, and manifested His glory; and His disciples believed in Him.

John 2:1-11

Luke's Gospel connects Jesus' return to Galilee and his Temptation by the devil, with the beginning of His ministry thus: "...in the power of the Holy Spirit, and news of him went out through all the surrounding region". (Lu 4:1-14) It is to get the attention of one and all, at this point in time, via of the miraculous transformation of water—something tasteless and very common— into a wonderful wine. That it was done in the power of the Holy Spirit, manifesting His glory and causing many to believe in him, is not just a coincidence. In the Amplified Bible, "manifesting His glory" is translated, "by it He displayed His greatness and His power openly, and His disciples believed in Him."

We could say: The miraculous, transforming power of *agape* love was put on open display in the context of matrimony, the best human love has to offer, in order to demonstrate to his servants that there is much more to "love" than meets the eye. While His glory manifests itself in many ways in this present world, first and foremost is in *agape* love...for God is love and love is of God. (1Jn 4:7,8,16)

The first of Jesus' miracles
displays the transforming power of Love—
the first order of His glory.

Pr. Tom Schaller:

The miracle of the water turned into wine at the wedding feast in Cana is one of my favorite Bible stories because it's a beautiful picture of the water of everyday life being transformed into the joy of the Lord. A person being born-again is also like water turned into wine.

The servants of the wedding feast were the only ones that actually knew a miracle had been performed; everyone else thought the bridegroom had broken the tradition of serving the best wine first. I have seen water turned into wine; every servant of our ministry has seen water turned into wine many times and, over the years, one of the greatest joys of my life has been to witness this miracle over and over again. I remember so well when our little church sent out its first missionary team to El Salvador; when we started a small Bible college in the basement of a Lutheran Church in Bath, Maine; when our bus ministry in Lenox, MA sent out forty-seven busses every Saturday morning to minister to hundreds of children in neighboring cities and communities. I remember servants walking by faith, Bible studies, and prayer meetings; many miracles of healing and deliverance are sweet memories to me. Yes, we have seen water turned into wine many times.

The servants who drew the water knew. People were drinking the wine, and they didn't know where it came from but the servants knew. The ones that filled the water pots; they knew. The ones that served the wedding guests were the ones who poured the wine out, and they were the *only* ones who knew an amazing miracle had taken place.

And I often reflect upon the work of our ministry because it is so edifying to me; Grace Hour being broadcast all over the world via satellite radio, Bible college students with a genuine fervent desire to follow Christ, Body-effort church-planting adventures, over 150 local outreaches, worldwide missions, men and women all over the world growing up in the faith.

Our calling is to fill the water pots with water, and we often don't know what's going to happen as we do; but this is the way we live—by faith, not by sight. These works are an outward, visible expression of something deep; I call it water—only water—but its water that is being transformed into wine! And as natural water is vital to biological life, this water is vital to spiritual life; it represents the water of the Word of God. This water is turned into wine, and only the servants know it, because they're the ones that live by the Word. One by one, two by two, here a little, there a little, a cupful here, a cupful there, servants fill the water pots to the brim and suddenly there's a miracle! Water becomes wine just as natural life in the world becomes supernatural life in the Spirit; rivers of living water (Jn 4:10-11, 7:38) are poured out from Heaven through His servants on earth.

Why do only the servants know it? Why is that they alone witness the works of God? Why is it that so many often do not recognize a work of God right before their eyes? Many simply do not regard it (Ps 28:5)— they do not consider or contemplate it in everyday life. Their lives are different from ours because we consider God's work continually in every area of life. We love the work of God; it's precious to us, the love of Christ constrains us, (2Co 5:14) it is a work of faith, and a labor of love. (1Th 1:3) We're witnesses to it, it has our hearts, or minds, and our focus at all times as we look for it everywhere, in everything, in everyone.

Neither does the natural man regard *agape* love. He is so taken up with loving the natural things of life, that he is deaf, dumb, and blind to the beauty of supernatural love. This love, which is intrinsic in God, is what we sometimes call objective Love, meaning God decided within Himself to love everyone personally, individually, and unconditionally, because He is love. (1Jo 4:8,16) Nothing can ever happen in anyone's life that can cancel out or discourage this love because God is immutable—absolutely unchanging, (Ma 3:6) and His love never fails (1Co 13:8) because He never fails.

The guests thoroughly enjoyed the wine even though they had no knowledge that it had been miraculously transformed from plain water. But the servants who knew of the miracle experienced a joy beyond the wine;

they experienced the transforming power of objective Love. The transformation of the water into wine was only a visible clue to an invisible, much, much greater miracle—the transformation that took place in the hearts of the servants.

The first priority of the new heart
is to serve the new wine
of objective love.

2

Objective Love Is
Absolutely Unconditional

God uses the life of Abraham and his son Isaac to teach many great truths, not the least of which is the unconditional nature of *objective Love*. When God releases His love to one who believes, that person instantly becomes an *object* of His love forever, and ever, and ever, and ever...*en ad infinitum*, and nothing, and nobody—not even the object—can change God's mind. (Mal 3:6)

This is a father/son relationship chosen to demonstrate a relationship between God and His only begotten Son at Calvary. (Ge 22:2)

Imagine you or I as Isaac—a teenager—having this testimony:

Father Abraham woke me up early in the morning to tell me we were going to Moriah to worship the Lord. We have morning worship often, but Mount Moriah? Why so far?

Everything was ready; the wood had been split and bundled, the donkey was loaded up, and two servants were ready to go with us. I didn't ask any questions, but I did wonder why we weren't taking a lamb. We had journeyed for three days when Father looked out to the horizon: There it is...Moriah, he said. He ordered the servants to stay with the donkey. Then he took the wood off the donkey and gave it to ME—another thing I didn't understand. I guess he thought I needed the exercise. But now, I had to ask, "...Father, what about the offering? Where's the lamb?"

Without hesitation he answered, "GOD will provide the offering!"

We trudged on in silence, up a rock-strewn hillside—not a likely place for worship if you ask me—but nobody did. We gathered some stones and made the altar, laid the wood on it, and I was looking around expecting to see a lamb appear...from somewhere. Then—without a word of explanation—Father took my hands and tied them behind me. And suddenly I understood! No, I thought! This can't be happening! I must be dreaming! He can't be serious! But then he tied my feet, picked me up, and laid me on the altar, and I knew he definitely was. I didn't say another word; I began to pray. And I was looking up into Father's tear filled eyes as he raised that same, sharp knife I've seen him use on many a sacrifice...I closed my eyes and took a deep breath. Not a word was spoken but my heart was crying out, "Father, into your hands I commit my spirit."

Amazing—at that point, I had no fear, only an awesome anticipation that when I next open my eyes I would be looking into the face of my Father in Heaven! I could feel the warmth of His love and, as I simply surrendered to it, in spite of these incredibly scary circumstances, all fear vanished—I was totally ready—to the point of being excited by just the thought seeing God.

And suddenly a loud voice—it seemed to come from everywhere: "ABRAHAM! ABRAHAM!"

Immediately I knew—it was the voice of the Lord!

"HERE AM I!" Father shouted.

Then God said, "Do not lay your hand on the lad, or do anything to him; for now I know that you fear God, since you have not withheld your son, your only son, from me." (Ge 22:12)

WHEW! Did my heart leap for joy, or what? Father cut the ropes binding my hands and feet; I was free, and I was off that altar—but quick!

Then there was the bleating of a sheep behind us! We turned to see a ram caught by its horns in a thicket. The offering! Awesome!! Father took it and sacrificed it—instead of me! Hallelujah! Praise Him! God is good!

One would think this experience would have equipped both Abraham and Isaac for anything the world, the flesh, or the devil could devise to divert them from the plan of God. But we are about to see how weak the flesh really is the instant it takes its eyes off the precious promises of Objective Love.

> There was a famine in the land, besides the first famine that was in the days of Abraham. And Isaac went to Abimelech king of the Philistines, in Gerar. Then the Lord appeared to him and said: "Do not go down to Egypt; live in the land of which I shall tell you. Dwell in this land, and I will be with you and bless you; for to you and your descendants I give all these lands, and I will perform the oath, which I swore to Abraham your father. And I will make your descendants multiply as the stars of heaven; I will give to your descendants all these lands; and in your seed all the nations of the earth shall be blessed; because Abraham obeyed My voice and kept My charge, My commandments, My statutes, and My laws." So Isaac dwelt in Gerar. And the men of the place asked about his wife. And he said, "She is my sister"; for he was afraid to say, "She is my wife," because he thought, "lest the men of the place kill me for Rebekah, because she is beautiful to behold."
>
> Genesis 26:1-7

God's promise to Isaac: "Dwell in the land that I will give to you, and I will be with you and bless you. I will give you and your descendants all countries. I will confirm the promise I made to your father, Abraham. (Ge 13:14-16) I will make your descendants more numerous than the stars in the sky, and through them all nations on earth will be blessed." (Ge 26:2-4)

In Genesis, the first book of the Bible, God is with Abraham and his seed, because Abraham believed. In Revelation, the last book of the Bible, God is in Heaven with all His people, people of every kindred, and tongue, and nation, because they believe. (Re 5:9, 14:6) God has been with all His people through all their experience on earth, all the way to Heaven, to bless them and make them a blessing, because they believe. A stone was anointed here, an altar was erected there, the Tabernacle was built, the Temple was built; Jesus Christ came to the earth, was crucified, died, buried, resurrected, and ascended back to his Father in Heaven. Now His tabernacle is with the redeemed here in this present world. Now, we who believe are His earthly temples: God dwells in us. (2Co 6:16)

There is an underlying theme in the Bible whereby God promises to dwell with people and bless them. Not all people; not all have the promise because not all believe. Abraham had it because he did believe. He had faith in God, and God counted his faith as righteousness. (Ge 15:5-6) He repeated this promise to Isaac, and Isaac's son, Jacob. He repeated it again to David, and his Son, Solomon, and David penned the promise given to The Messiah. (Ps 2:8) We could say this promise is like the Gospel, even the Old Testament Gospel. At the end of the Bible Jesus finally confirms the promise made to all his disciples. (Re 22:5)

On his way out of the land of Ur, Abraham sojourned in Egypt. He was a foreigner there, and in those days you needed to be very careful in a foreign country, so Abraham would be insecure—even a little frightened—but God had promised to make his name great, to bless him, and make him a blessing to all nations, and to give him all countries. Yet, when he met the king of Gerar, he was fearful because his wife, Sarah, was very beautiful and he was sure the king would desire her, and kill him to have her; therefore, he told the king she was his sister. Sure enough, the king actually did take her, but God appeared to him in a dream and told him the truth about Sarah, that he would lose everything—including his life—if he did not immediately return her to Abraham. (Ge 20:1-7) Needless to say, she was immediately returned!

Now, we find Isaac in Gerar where God appeared to him with the same promise. And isn't it interesting that Isaac finds himself in a predicament identical to that of his father? This teaches us that His promises are unfailing as they reach across and apply to all generations. And what does Isaac do when the pressure is on? Exactly the same thing his father did; he tells the very same lie!

Abraham was a believer, but he was also a liar, and so was Isaac. Nevertheless, God's decision was that he would love them with objective Love that would never fail even though their love would. No matter how miserably the object of God's love fails, objective Love never fails; (1 Co 13:8) this love is the essence of a covenant God made with His people, in His own heart—with Himself—because He could swear by no one greater. (He 6:13) Actually, the Father said to the Son, "Sit thou at my right hand, until I make thine enemies thy footstool." (Ps 110:1)

> If his sons forsake my law And do not walk in my judgments, If they break my statutes and do not keep my commandments, Then I will punish their transgression with the rod, and their iniquity with stripes. Nevertheless my loving-kindness I will not utterly take from him, nor allow my faithfulness to fail. My covenant I will not break, nor alter the word that has gone out of my lips. Once I have sworn by my holiness; I will not lie to David:
>
> Psalm 89:30-35

This is the way it is with us—as it was with our fathers before us: When the pressure is on, if our hearts take one step outside of objective Love, fear takes over and human reasoning rules with self-preservation at all costs, but objective Love is perfect love, and perfect love casts out fear [1Jo 4:18] and makes the coward to be courageous. Human love is not perfect and cannot do this, but objective Love is made perfect through human love, that we may have boldness on Judgment Day. [1Jo 4:17-18] Now, I can't imagine anything more fearful than Judgment Day, but if I actually believe, when judgment does come, Christ's objective Love will work through human love, and I will have a holy boldness before Him in perfected Love. This most amazing manifestation of objective Love will glorify and bless God and all of Heaven forever. Hallelujah!

So we say, "Isaac, what are you saying? What are you thinking? Weren't you listening, Isaac? Didn't you hear the promise? Don't you believe it? This is a Love covenant—objective Love, Isaac! And you're behaving like a coward!"

But do you or I ever fail in this way? Do we ever feel empty? Are we ever embarrassed? Do we tell lies in situations—especially "little white lies"? Do we ever try to make ourselves look better than we really are in the eyes of our peers? Are we ever jealous of others? Do people ever make us angry or depressed? Do we ever purposely avoid certain people? Do we ever hunger for love to the point of being...desperate? Of course we all do; we all have these feelings at times. It's an experience common to every soul, and it's called subjectivity—what we personally experience. And it's not entirely wrong; there is bona fide subjectivity that is healthy, but there is subjectivity that isn't healthy at all because it deceives us and misleads.

On a given day our emotions cry out: "Doesn't anybody love me?" But we go to the Covenant and say, "Wait a minute! God has chosen me. I'm in a covenant of Love with God who actually IS love. He wants to make my name great. I'm a citizen of a great nation—the Kingdom of God. He indwells every fiber of my being... and I AM LOVED."

Now I'm being subjective, but I'm also encouraging myself in the Lord [1Sa 30:6] with objective Love; there's nothing wrong with this kind of subjectivity.

Or else, out of the abundance of my heart, Isaac—my fallen nature—speaks: "Oh, yeah! I know all about that, but this is what my feelings are going through right now: FEAR! I'm just a little *fearful* that this need might not be met! Sorry! This time I need to take matters into my own hands...I know God understands. Would He expect me to just DIE? Not protect myself??"

This is subjectivity at it's worst, and now Isaac's conscience speaks with conviction: "Isaac, if you walked in objective Love, if you knew the person of God, if you walked in the fellowship of the promise, if you lived by faith and not by sight, if you knew the Holy Spirit is eager and desiring to anoint you and fill you, then you would speak like this: That woman? She's my wife! Isn't she beautiful? I am so blessed! Hey, here's more! God promised my father and I that our family will become a great nation, that He will dwell with us, and never leave us or forsake us. [He 13:5] By the way, He gave us eternal life also! And...by the way, the God we worship created the entire universe and you and I and every living thing—starting with nothing! And...by the way, all the promises of God are Yea, and Amen unto the glory of God by us. [2Co 1:20] ...Yep! She's awesome! And she IS my wife! Isn't God great? And... by the way, my God would love to be your God! How about it? You could pray me and receive Him into your life right now."

Isaac could have easily covered this situation— and his wife—with objective Love; by receiving it and trusting it do its work. His faith would have been a great testimony and encouragement to all, but he let his *feelings* usurp authority over his soul, and *fear* became the dictator of his decisions: "Careful now, Isaac. You could really get into trouble here. The King might want

Rebekah for himself. Yeah! Right! Over our dead body, of course!" And his response to the king's question was: "Yes, O King! She's only my sister! By the way...would you like to meet her, Your Royal Highness?"

But have I ever had an experience like this? Have I ever felt that kind of fear, or embarrassment, or shame? I have! And I pray: "Yes, Lord. I am afraid—of myself, because I know you're promises are great. Though my flesh is weak, you're Spirit in me is willing. I believe that your Son not only came into history, but even into me personally. I believe that He died for me, and all my sins, that He was buried, resurrected, and ascended back to Heaven. Lord, I do believe; please help my unbelief!"

We have read these things in His Word and it is quite clear to us but of course ancient men of faith like Abraham, Isaac, and Jacob didn't have the theology of the New Testament. We have it, we know it, and we have amazing understanding of what it means to live in the New Covenant promises. When we read the Old Testament we see beyond the Word to the spirit of the Word because we see objective Love.

Why should Isaac fear the King of Gerar? What about the promises? Could he have forgotten that awesome day on Mount Moriah so soon? No, That's not the problem! The problem is that Isaac, in a situation that challenges his faith, does not choose to receive Love, and this is often what we all do in trials of our faith. Confronted with difficult decisions we find that we're only human and we always have that potential to default to our fallen nature.

The object of God's love
is ever failing...
but Objective Love
never fails.

2

Objective Love Is Sovereign

> Now it came to pass, when he had been there a long time, that Abimelech king of the Philistines looked through a window, and saw, and there was Isaac, showing endearment to Rebekah his wife.
>
> Genesis 26:8

There's always somebody looking out the window! The king caught Isaac and Rebekah showing endearment (the King James Version calls it "sporting"). Abimelech is thinking: "Oh-Oooooo! Sisters and brothers don't play around like that! I'll bet she's his wife! He lied to me! No guts, no courage! He's a liar!"

There's always someone there to find out the truth about us. The Bible says we can be sure of it—*your sins will find you out.* [(Nu 32:23)] And when they do, we're embarrassed and ashamed, and well we should be, but be sure of this also: Our sin does NOT change the covenant of Love!

> Then Abimelech called Isaac and said, "Quite obviously she is your wife; so how could you say, 'She is my sister?'" Isaac said to him, "Because I said, 'Lest I die on account of her.'"
>
> Verse 9

Isaac's thoughts: I wouldn't want to die for her, Your Highness! God forbid that I die for my wife!
My thoughts: Isaac! You remind me so much of myself. O, Isaac! I hear my own subjective heart speaking to me: "Not me! No way! You want me to get in trouble here; you want me to die?

61

> And Abimelech said, "What is this you have done to us?
> One of the people might soon have lain with your wife,
> and you would have brought guilt on us." So Abimelech
> charged all his people, saying, "He who touches this
> man or his wife shall surely be put to death." Then
> Isaac sowed in that land, and reaped in the same year a
> hundredfold; and the Lord blessed him.

Verses 10-12

Wait a minute; I thought Isaac lied! Yes, he did lie! But can God bless His own people in any way He wants, whenever He so desires? If a liar sows in a field, and is blessed with a hundredfold harvest, who are we to contest God's grace? Who are we to say God can't give grace and do as He pleases with what is His? If He made a covenant with Isaac, and desires to bless him, and does so, who are we to judge God? And does this mean that we just tell a lie if we think we need to? Is it all right to break The Commandment? Is it all right to bear false witness against a neighbor? No! No! NO! God forbid it! God forbid it if sin abounds that grace might much more abound. (Ro 5:12) That simply is NOT the way it is. THIS is the way it is: The last thing Love ever wants to do is hurt Love!

Don't we see your own humanity in this story? Don't we see ourselves, and our sin? Can I not imagine myself squirming, feeling uncomfortable, and being ashamed in this situation? Do I not see God dealing with me, correcting me, disciplining me in Love, and mercy that endures forever? (Ps 136) Do I not see sovereign, objective Love in action? Yes, I truly do! And I praise Him!

Isaac sowed in the land of Gerar, and reaped a hundredfold; God blessed him in spite of his lies and deceit; that's called sovereign objective Love! I will bless you; do you hear me? I have saved you; do you understand? You have eternal life; do you know that? All your sins are washed away; do you realize that? Your name is written in the Book Of Life, in indelible Blood;

you can't change that even if you want to; do you believe this? Rejoice then! Rejoice that your name is written in Heaven. (Lu 10:20)

This is the covenant of sovereign, objective Love that God made with His only begotten Son, and the Holy Spirit when He determined that, the instant we believe, we receive all spiritual blessings in Heavenly places, in Christ Jesus, (Ep 1:3) even while we were yet sinners. (Ro 5:8) We have received it; it's all there, that's the promise of God, and it can't be changed—that's the way it is—and that's why we call it, *the finished work.*

> *Somebody:* But then the grace of God leads us into sin!
> *Me*: No way, the same grace that saves us teaches us NOT to sin. (Ti 2:11-12)

Objective Love is sovereign and has its source in sovereign grace. Isaac's story is encouraging to me because I see myself in his place, and I say to myself, "Come on, Isaac! Come on now! Stand! Stand under the pressure of the flesh, stand in grace, stand in objective Love, Isaac. Of course you don't deserve it but, after all, that's what grace is—a manifestation of Love we don't deserve."

The same is true for all of us; we're encouraged to live in His love, we're encouraged to Love one another, not based upon what we do, or what we don't do, but upon what Christ has already done. We don't love a person based upon whether we like them or not; that's subjective! We don't love someone when it's convenient; that's subjective! We don't love someone because we feel like it on Monday—but not on Sunday! That's subjective love. We Love as God loves us; that's objective Love—Covenant Love in action—and we Love one another with His Love; that's perfected Love!

If we go through the Bible page, by page, by page, from cover to cover, we see promise, upon promise, upon promise, upon promise—nearly eight thousand of them, and not a single one will fall to the ground; ever! They're all, yea, and in Him, Amen! (2Co 1:20) What God has decided in Himself is absolute, sovereign, objective grace and truth that cannot fail because it is based upon Love that never fails.

Yes, He deals with us! Yes, He chastises us when we sin; but it's always in objective Love that never changes, never fails, never leaves us or forsakes us, and always loves us unconditionally. Our names are written in the Book Of Life, (Re 3:5) we're sealed in the Holy Spirit, (2Co 1:22) and we may have a tendency to sin because we still do have a sin nature, but we can choose to live in objectivity, in doctrine, through the Cross, submitted to Him, by faith. When we do we will assuredly experience the power of Love never failing, because we're living in sovereign, objective Love.

Pr. Tom Schaller:

In times past, many of our Pastors—myself included—really didn't want to become Pastors. I personally felt that I wasn't equipped for it and I didn't even really have the desire; I wanted to run the other away, which is exactly what we all do if we allow our subjective self to rule over our life. But instead, we set our sights upon Love, objective Love, and the nature of God. Even to our own hurt we follow Him and discover, not our own faithfulness, but His faithfulness working in us. Then we see water turned into wine—miracles of transformation—and we ask, "How did this ever happen; how did I get here; how did I ever become...a Pastor?" But we realize that human love met objective Love, and the result was spontaneous—perfected Love. We didn't do it; God did it, and His servants knew He did it! It wasn't our choice, it was His leading; and of course our free volition had to choose, but still, it's Him who works in us *both to will and to do his good pleasure.* (Php 2:12-13) We see the promises fulfilled in us, we see objective Love in action, and we're absolutely sure we could NOT do it...Objective Love did it in us and through us.

> *Objective love transforms the water of*
> *subjective love.*
> *into the wine of*
> *perfected Love.*

Chapter 3
— Agape Love —

Childlike Faith

At that time the disciples came to Jesus, saying, "Who then is greatest in the kingdom of heaven?" Then Jesus called a little child to Him, set him in the midst of them, and said, "Assuredly, I say to you, unless you are converted and become as little children, you will by no means enter the kingdom of heaven. Therefore whoever humbles himself as this little child is the greatest in the kingdom of heaven. Whoever receives one little child like this in my name receives me.

Matthew 18:1-5

In this text Jesus is teaching his disciples the importance of having the heart and mindset of a child, which is typically one of humility. We could define humility, in a spiritual sense, simply as a knowing that we always need God; without Him we can do nothing. (Jn 15:5) And humility is the mother of meekness, a willingness to always be submitted to God's plan and purpose. If we are truly humble we are also truly meek. How does meekness and humility relate to faith? Meekness demands a child-like faith, and children are Heaven's emblems of humility, meekness, and faith in God, because they always need to be loved unconditionally, and are ever receptive to Love. Jesus' love for his disciples will change their lives forever; they will be converted and become as little children: humble, meek, and full of child-like faith.

Have you noticed? Truly great men and women of ministry are as little children before God. I have a friend who is gifted and anointed in wisdom, leadership, and decision-making. I have known him for nearly thirty years and have been a witness many times to his greatness in the Kingdom of Heaven. Recently we were having a private prayer meeting (I had been reading Matthew 18) and as he began to pray I was immediately reminded of how, with all his greatness as a minister of Jesus Christ and the Gospel, he is totally child-like before the Lord.

Jesus also uses the occasion of this teaching to stress the importance of an attitude of unconditional love and respect for children. (Verses 5-10) Regardless of what we see to the contrary in a world that often victimizes them, Jesus assures us: "Their angels do always behold the face of my Father in Heaven." (Verse 10)—which is comforting to know in this present world, and I am sure it was when Jesus spoke those words. But there is also an application here to believers; we are children, in the eyes of our Heavenly Father. And we're often taken advantage of because of our faith, and humility, but we're never without angelic covering. This also, is a comforting thing to know.

> For the Son of man is come to save that which was lost.
>
> Verse 11

The first word of this verse connects it to the preceding text; the subject has not changed. Spiritually speaking, the unsaved—and even the saved that lack spiritual leadership, teaching, and training—are as lost children. These are the lost coins, lost sheep, and lost sons of Luke 15. A disciple will always need child-like receptivity to the love of God because spiritual warfare will always be a major part of the Christian experience. We are as sheep—or we might say, little children—among wolves.
(Mt 10:16, Lu 10:3)

Receiving Love and giving Love, being Loved and Loving others, letting God's love minister to us, and ministering His love to others, is ever the process of Love holding the line against the enemies of our soul.

Who then is the greatest in the Kingdom of Heaven?
What do you think?
Whoever will humble himself as a little child is the greatest in the Kingdom of Heaven.

3

What do you think?

> What do you think? If a man has a hundred sheep, and one of them goes astray, does he not leave the ninety-nine and go to the mountains to seek the one that is straying?
>
> Matthew 18:12

Jesus is very skillful at searching hearts. [1Ch 16:9] He asks, "What do you think? If a man has a hundred sheep..." and "What do you think? A certain man had two sons..." [Mt 21:28] and "What do you think of Christ? Whose Son is he?" [Mt 22:42] And why is it that what we're thinking is so important to him? It is because what we're thinking actually reveals who we are. [Pr 23:7] Jesus knows the hearts of men; He knows that, without Love, his Disciples have no capacity to seek the one lost sheep that strays from the flock; therefore, he is ever searching hearts for receptivity to Love. [2Ch 16:9] Who is with him on the issue of lost children? What are our priorities on a day-to-day basis? Do we recognize our need to operate in *agape* love in every detail of life? If we do not, we're easily prone to being deceived by our emotions, our wants and needs (our own as well as those of others), the world system, and—last, but not least—principalities, ...powers, ...the rulers of the darkness of this world, ... spiritual wickedness in high places. [Ep 6:12]

Life is about making decisions, and every decision in life really is a Kingdom decision; either it benefits the Kingdom of God, or it benefits the kingdom of darkness. If we're not with him, we're against him; if we're not gathering, we're scattering. [Mt 12:30, Lu 11:23] Divine love always works through human love to inspire Kingdom priorities;

(Mt 6:33) Loving God with all our heart, with all our soul, and with our entire mind; (Mt 22:37) seeking and saving the lost; (Lu 19:10) global missions taking the Gospel into all the world; (Mt 28:19-20, Ac 1:8)...Loving one another as he Loves us. (Jn 13:34, 15:12, 17) When *agape* love works through us we see beyond the subjectivity and sentimentality of autonomous, human thought, we begin to see everything and everyone with the eyes and mind of Christ. (1 Co 2:16) We have the right first priority and every other priority automatically falls into its proper place, (Mt 6:33-34) and demons flee away from us as fast as they can go (which is at least Warp I). (Ja 4:7)

I may think I'm the greatest in the Kingdom because of my theology, or my religious works, or my morality, or my heritage, or my anything; but if I lack child-like faith I'm ill-equipped to receive God's love. Without it I am nothing (1Co 13:2-3) and I will not even enter into the Kingdom of Heaven, (Mat 18:3) never mind be the greatest one there! This is why Jesus said to Nicodemus, a respected leader among the very religious Pharisees, You must be born again. (Jn 3:3-8) The instant I'm born-again, God gives me a new heart and a new spirit divinely equipped with *agape* love, (Ez 18:31, 36:26; Ro 5:5) from which all other spiritual gifts—joy, peace, longsuffering, gentleness, goodness, faith, meekness, and temperance—have their source. (Ga 5:22-23)

It is absolutely essential for the new heart to be filled with Love (Ro 5:5) for it must be equipped with divine power (Greek: *dunamis*) in order to function in the Kingdom of Heaven on Planet Earth, and beyond—even into eternity!

> ...As His divine power has given to us all things that pertain to life and godliness, through the knowledge of Him who called us by glory and virtue...
>
> 2 Peter 1:3

"Divine power" is interpreted from the Greek, *dunamis*: miracle-working power—the same power the

Disciples were promised at Pentecost, ^(Ac 1:8) the same power every believer receives when born of the Spirit.

"Knowledge of Him" that calls us is that experiential knowledge which reveals the power of His great love for us. ^(Ep 2:4)

The five essential functions of the mind—thinking, remembering, knowing, understanding, and imagining—are energized by Love, and the new heart has the ability to shed spiritual light upon every area of our soul; mind, emotions, volition, conscience, self-consciousness, and even the subconscious.

The miracle-working power of perfect love that comes through knowledge of him to the life of every believer cannot be overestimated.

"What do you think?" Jesus asks. "A certain man had an hundred sheep, and he lost one...And he left the ninety-nine and went looking for the one."

What do you think of that? How do you judge this matter? Did he do the right thing? What would you do? His question is intended to carefully—and graciously—search our hearts, challenge every mental function to think with him, without destroying our capacity to learn of him. This is very important because we live in a world that has many false concepts about God, and about many other things in life, and especially about "love". These concepts need to be challenged, but it must be challenged with great care not to destroy a capacity to receive Love by overwhelming someone with religious works and/or legalism. The disciple must learn Love's methodology well because it is the key to the Great Commission—seeking and saving the lost, teaching, and making disciples.

Love is the skillful heart of a fisher-of-men,
fine-tuned
to the gracious heart of God.

> Then Paul stood in the midst of the Areopagus and said, "Men of Athens, I perceive that in all things you are very religious; for as I was passing through and considering the objects of your worship, I even found an altar with this inscription: TO THE UNKNOWN GOD. Therefore, the One whom you worship without knowing, Him I proclaim to you...
>
> Acts 17:22-23

Now, Paul could have rebuked the men of Athens for outright idolatry—what true Christian wouldn't? But, no! He very graciously used the occasion to get their attention by—of all things—acknowledging their idol! (Now, would that be a turn-off to a hyper-spiritual, Pharisee person, or what?) But then he preached the Gospel of Jesus Christ to them, proclaiming Him to actually be the unknown God they worshipped. Yes, some mocked Paul, but some did believe, and were saved, and actually became Paul's disciples. (Ac 17:32-34)

It's all-important to have a new heart and a new spirit, but it's also important to have a mind filled with doctrine—instruction in truth (God's Word). (Jn 17:17) Our ministry teaches doctrine in categories—collections of scripture that correlate with one another on any given topic or subject; we call it *categorical doctrine*. Categorical doctrine equips us to think with God in categories of truth. Truth is a powerful, precision tool of *agape* love. We speak the truth in Love. (Ep 4:14-15)

Three books in the Bible—I & II Timothy, and Titus—teach Timothy, the Pastor, the importance of categorical doctrine being taught to every believer; this is vitally important to our total being—body, soul, and spirit. (1Th 5:23) Every day of our life we deal with questions and make decisions that defy human understanding and logic, we face trials and tribulations without number, we have enemies that seek to destroy our soul (many of which are invisible), we have concepts of God that need correction, and we have a sin nature. Therefore, we desperately need to learn to let God love us; then we can love Him, ourselves, one another, and even our enemies, as the Word of God says we must. Like the proverbial camel going through the eye of a needle, this seems impossible at times, but because of the miracle working power of *agape* love working in us, it assuredly is possible. (Mt 19:23-26, Mk 10:27)

*Doctrine is the door
of discipleship,
and Love is the key to that door —
but child-like faith
turns the key.*

3

Think No Evil

The unsaved are caught-up in a terrible dilemma: Hurting from the consequences of sin, often a victim of the sins of others, burdened with guilt and shame, having many difficult questions with few real answers, they are surrounded from within and without by enemies of the soul. And it doesn't end there: Ruled-over by a sin nature—a heart that is unpredictable, unstable, insecure, double minded, (Ja 1:8) self-serving, and deceitful above all things, (Je 17:5-9) they are alienated from God. (Ep 2:12) Totally dependent upon the natural senses and physical world, (1Jn 2:16) they are often under the spell of spirits (Ep 6:12, 1Pe 5:8) specializing in using worldliness as a tool to manipulate human thought. In the midst of all these negatives, few have a clue as to cause and effect. And Jesus would say, as he hung on the Cross: "Father, forgive them, for they do know not what they do..." (Lu 23:34) What amazing Love this is!

When all the Jews were gathered together Pilate asked, "What do you think? (Familiar words?) Who should I release to you? Barabbas, or Jesus?" (Mt 27:15-25) Now, would this be a difficult decision for you or I? What do you think? And we might answer, "...Easy!" But if we project ourselves into the place of people who were actually there, faced with that dread decision, the first thing we realize is that we have no doctrine. Our religious teachers have not prepared us for this. Contrariwise, they purposely turned our hearts against him? (Mt 27:20) So much so, that we're willing to release a convicted criminal—one guilty of robbery and murder—into the very midst of us instead of him who is guilty of nothing but Loving us. Now it's not easy for me to picture myself as a 1st Century Jew living in Roman occupied Judea, but I can easily picture myself without doctrine because it wasn't all that long ago that I actually was without doctrine, and I know that, back in those days, I could very easily get caught up in a mob mentality. I confess that I've even been guilty of doing so, i.e. at a silly Yankee—Red Sox baseball game. Oh, my! But who hasn't??

Who will we choose to release? Barabbas, or Jesus? What do you think?

We all shout, "GIVE US BARABBAS!"
"And what shall I do with this Jesus, who is called Christ?" asks Pilate.
"LET HIM BE CRUCIFIED!"
"Why? What evil has he done?"
"CRUCIFY HIM! CRUCIFY HIM! CRUCIFY HIM!" we chant.
And finally Pilate literally washes his hands before us, and proclaims, "I am innocent of the blood of this just person! See to it!"
And we all shout it out: "LET HIS BLOOD BE ON US AND ON OUR CHILDREN!"

Is our sin nature a wicked thing, or what? How could we say such a thing; how do we make one bad decision after another? But we can and we do, more often than we think—even if we're saved.

Their hearts were utterly unable to see divine light, unable to know the mind of God, (Is 55:8-9, 65:2) because they did not have doctrine. And if we're not saved—or even if we are—and don't have doctrine, we're not one iota less prone to wickedness and deception than were the very people who shouted, "CRUCIFY HIM! CRUCIFY HIM! CRUCIFY HIM!" But if we are saved and we do have doctrine, we are well able to think with God in every situation. "What do you think?" is indeed a very good question.

> [Agape] does not behave rudely, does not seek its own,
> is not provoked, thinks no evil...
>
> 1 Corinthians 13:5

How does Love in the new heart of a believer manifest itself? It manifests itself through the process of thought, which produces action. *Agape* thinks! *Agape* thinks no evil; it remembers no evil, it knows no evil, it understands no evil, and it imagines no evil. The five functions of the mental process, under the influence of *agape*, know absolutely nothing but perfect Love, and that's what they always think. What do you and I think?

God desires for us to have truth (doctrine) in our inward parts. (Ps 51:6) Inward parts, is translated from the Hebrew, *tuwchah*: the inmost thought, or the center of the thought process—the mind. *Agape* is manifested through doctrine that has been assimilated—integrated into, or absorbed—by the mind, the thought center of the heart. Truth in the inward parts actually makes it possible for *agape* to think.

Contrasting *agape* is autonomous, human love—*philos* (soulish) love, which is manifested, not through the mind, but through the emotions. Human love only feels: I love you...I love Coffee...I love Lucy...I love my friends...I love my house...but I hate housekeeping...I love to ride in my new car...but I hate the traffic. These words express feelings—emotional, sentimental, or romantic feelings. And that may be all right, but do they reveal the mind of God? If not, they reveal the mind of the natural man who cannot think with God; (1Co 2:14) this heart will consistently make judgments and decisions based upon subjectivity and self-preservation. But if human love does reveal God's mind, it's because it's thinking with Him—operating in one accord with *agape*.

With *agape* love, doctrine always dominates the thought process; with human love, feelings dominate thought if they can't access truth. Human love actually can access truth, but only if/when truth is resident in the mind, and it operates in accord with Love. This is "love" by divine design—perfected Love. The dilemma of a heart that cannot access truth is that God didn't give us emotions for the purpose of thinking; they're purpose is to respond to truth with feeling, not human rationalization and sentimentality detached from truth. In the absence of truth in the inward parts, in a situation that requires Loving response, the heart of the natural man defaults to subjectivity— thinking based upon personal feelings only.

"What do you think?" Jesus asks—and he's very interested in how his Disciples think, because they have a Heavenly call upon their lives [He 3:1] to seek and to save the lost; [Lu 19:10, Jn 20:21] they're ambassadors for Christ, [2Co 5:20] ministers of righteousness, [2Co 11:5] stewards of the mysteries of God, [1Co 4:1] called with a high calling, [Php 3:14] and with a holy calling before ever the world began [2Ti 1:9]—and so are you and I.

Someone without doctrine will say:

"I won't go there; I just don't feel like it..."

"I don't like this message. It doesn't make me feel good, and I am not going to receive it—No way..."

"I know I should minister to him, but there's something about him that I really don't like..."

"I should go soul winning but I don't like being rejected by people. I really don't know the Bible all that well..."

"I used to love her, but not any more. It's over!"

These statements reveal a mind void of truth, and emotions dominating and manipulating thinking and the decision making process. This love is entirely soulish—double minded, not connected to *agape*, undependable, deceitful, self serving, and incapable of keeping commitments—because the heart behind it is totally unable to send light (spiritual illumination) into the mind. The depths of this soul are dark; they've experienced injury, feelings were hurt, emotions are wounded, and now they do the thinking. *Agape* isn't thinking, emotions are! When the emotions dominate the mental process—thinking, remembering, knowing, understanding, and imagining—with human love, they always cause the soul to make decisions outside of God's plan and purpose. When a doctrine filled mind is energized by a new heart and *agape* love, it causes the soul to think with God, enabling it to make decisions with Kingdom priorities. (Mt 6:33-34)

> *Love patiently teaches us*
> *all things*
> *pertaining to life and Godliness,*
> *until we think*
> *no evil whatsoever.*

3

A Form Of Godliness

Truth will deliver us from the power of darkness and translate us into the Kingdom of His dear Son; (Cu 1.10-13) it will also transform us into children of light, (Ep 5:8, 1Th 5:5) and set us free, (Jn 8:32) but only if we don't allow our feelings to have dominion over our decision-making. So we think with the *agape* love of the new heart—in a new and living way (He 10:20) ...or we think with our old, sin nature:

> But know this, that in the last days perilous times will come: For men will be lovers of themselves, lovers of money, boasters, proud, blasphemers, disobedient to parents, unthankful, unholy, unloving, unforgiving, slanderers, without self-control, brutal, despisers of good, traitors, headstrong, haughty, lovers of pleasure rather than lovers of God, having a form of godliness but denying its power. And from such people turn away! For of this sort are those who creep into households and make captives of gullible women loaded down with sins, led away by various lusts, always learning and never able to come to the knowledge of the truth.
>
> 2 Timothy 3:1-7

Paul is warning Pastor Timothy that end times will be characterized by amazing evil and deception...even in the Church. We know end times are already upon us because much of the above is evident in this present world. Jesus himself warns that the Love [*agape*—love common only to believers] of many will grow cold because iniquity will abound in the last days. (Mt 24:12)

We always try to minister grace and believe the best of everyone, but we do know that many have a form of godliness without divine power. Jesus said: "By their fruits you will know them." (Mt 7:15-20)

79

Sometimes I refuse to simply let God love me because I feel that I don't deserve to be loved—especially by God. And indeed I do not, but the glory of the Gospel is that He loves me anyway. All I need do is humble my heart and believe that Christ cleared the way of all the rubbish standing between God and myself, by the Blood of his Cross—the Finished Work. (Jn 19:30) And if I don't do this my emotions immediately want to take over, but I purposely pray, receive Love, and meditate upon the Cross, and it is amazing how faithful the Holy Spirit is to comfort me, and absolutely check my actions.

Sometimes a refusal to let God love me has its roots in pride—my heart's desire to be self-sufficient—its own source—so I learn doctrine with my intellectual mind, and apply it to others, but there is never an application to my own heart; therefore, I never become rooted and grounded in Love. (Ep 3:17) I know truth but its only knowledge—never becomes truth in the inward parts— and it cannot set me, or anyone else, free; I appear to be spiritual but I'm really only religious. God's word concerning those who purpose to know doctrine but consistently refuse to live in it is: "From such people turn away! (2Tm 3:5) By their fruits you will know them." (Mt 7:15-20)

A form of godliness may actually have ungodly power. This is power that destroys using subjective love under the auspices of objective Love; it is a diabolical counterfeit having the outward appearance of Godliness but when it counts for the Kingdom, what you see is not what you get. Characteristic of what the Bible calls *iniquity*, this singular sin is the direct result of wounded emotions that dominate a normal thought process.

Iniquity was first found in Lucifer, the anointed cherub (angel), (Ez 28:14-16) when he learned that God's plan was to redeem fallen human beings and exalt them above angels. (Ps 8:5) Pride took Lucifer's heart; self-deception followed immediately and led to outright rebellion among the angels [Isa 14:12-14] and the fall of one third of them. [Re 12:4] The fall of Adam and Eve followed soon afterwards when Satan (Lucifer's new name, meaning, adversary) somehow assumed the form of a serpent, approached Eve with lies about God, [Ge 3:1-5] and actually got her to believe God was lying to her. The seeds of iniquity were sown; Eve carried them to Adam with a form of godliness having power to wound his emotions with the pain of losing her, and she verily did wound him. The fall of humanity was complete at that instant. Satan had already become—then was, and now is—the DIABOLICAL WIZARD of all time, whose forte ever is the culmination of the corrupted wisdom of the ages: *iniquity.* Jesus' warning rings true in this present world and in much of the Christianity today: "And because iniquity shall abound, the Love of many shall wax cold." [Mt 24:12]

We're thankful to God that He doesn't deal with us after our sins, or reward us according to our iniquities. [Ps 103:10] Blessed are they whose iniquities are forgiven, and whose sins are covered [Ro 4:7]...by Love! [1Pe 4:8]

> Now as Jannes and Jambres resisted Moses, so do these also resist the truth: men of corrupt minds, disapproved concerning the faith; but they will progress no further, for their folly will be manifest to all, as theirs also was.
>
> Verse 8-9

Jannes and Jambres were the Egyptian magicians who tried to neutralize the miracles of Moses, which were performed before Pharaoh; they succeeded for a while but ultimately failed totally. [Ex 7:1-8:19] God may allow deception to test hearts, and the authority of truth will always be resisted by unbelief, but ultimately no weapon formed against truth will stand. [Is 54:17] This is why, rooted and grounded in Love, God always gives us the victory [1Co 15:57] and we're more than conquerors through him that Loved us. [Ro 8:37] Can we really believe these precious promises yet today? Yes, indeed we can, because God created the material universe—things seen and things unseen—with truth as its essence; every attempt to undermine it is, therefore, sheer folly (Greek, *anoiai*: stupidity; or madness). One might as well try to resist gravity—jump over the moon—as resist truth.

Many have heard of the feats of the late Evel Kneival (1938-2007). Evel was well known for—let us say—testing the law of gravity. In September 1974 he tried to ride a homemade rocket over Snake River Grand Canyon, which is about 1600 feet across and 600 feet deep. The entire world was watching as he attempted this daring stunt and his folly was manifested to all men because soon after his rocket was launched it crashed into the opposite wall of the canyon. Evel did progress no further... and actually was fished out of the Snake River. We thank God that his life was spared (with minor injuries) but his pride surely was not.

Recently at a Palm Sunday service in The Crystal Cathedral, in Garden Grove, CA, Evel gave a testimony of how he steadfastly refused to accept Jesus Christ as his Savior for sixty-eight years. He believed in God—of course—but he said he "...couldn't walk away from all the gold, and the gambling, and the booze, and the women...I don't know what in the world happened. I don't know if it was the power of the prayer, or God himself, but it just reached out, either while I was driving, or walking down the sidewalk, or sleeping, or it just—the power of God in Jesus just grabbed me...All of a sudden, I just believed in Jesus Christ. I did, I believed in him! I rose up in bed and—I was by myself—and I said, 'Devil! Devil, you bastard you, get away from me! I cast you out of my life!'...I just got on my knees and prayed that God would put his arms around me and never, ever, ever let me go."

He asked to be baptized then and there, and he was, which triggered a mass-baptism that continued into a second service, and about 800 people were baptized and/or re-dedicated their lives to Christ! Christianity Today; (05/30/07)

There is no substitute for truth in our mind; we are created for truth, (Ja 1:18) and we are hopelessly lost without it. It is fundamental to our very existence; any attempt to subvert it in our life is the great folly of the created in the face of the Creator. We could define sin simply as every attempt we make to contradict truth. Every second of our life without the Lord Jesus Christ—the way, the truth, and the life—might as well be a rocket ride across the Snake River Grand Canyon. Sheer folly! And often we escape with minor injuries, but not always.

We're so instructed to encourage us to give the Word of Truth (2Co 6:7, Ep 1:13, Co 1:5) top priority in our life. Jesus said, "Heaven and earth shall pass away, but my words [truth] shall not pass away." (Mt 24:35, Mk 13:31, Lu 21:33)

But you have carefully followed my doctrine...

Verse 10

The Amplified Bible version reads:

"Now you have closely observed and diligently followed my teaching, conduct, purpose in life, faith, patience, and love..."

Verse 10 (Amp)

To fully know Paul's doctrine means that Timothy not only heard it, he lived it—diligently followed it—proved it out in his life and experienced it—until he possessed it and was possessed by it. Paul's teaching became Timothy's life, transformed his mind and his mental process, (Ro 12:2) and fitted him for Love made perfect. We cannot possibly have a higher purpose in this life... and we certainly will not in the next, which will be forever and ever.

*In the measure that I possess truth,
and am possessed by truth,
is the measure that I am successful
in this life,
and glorious in Heaven.*

3

Wisdom's House

Wisdom has built her house, She has hewn out her
seven pillars...

Proverbs 9:1

In six days, starting with nothing, God created the
totality of the material universe, including even you and
I. Some may want to correct me and say, "Well, at least
He created Adam and Eve at that time." And I would say,
"We were absolutely present, naturally speaking, in the
genetic pool Adam and Eve contained. And spiritually
speaking we were already present in His omniscient,
eternal mind anyway. (Rom 8:29-30) His work was finished
and complete—and on the seventh day He rested—
interpreted from the original Hebrew, *shabath*: sat
down and sat still. (Ge 2:3) therefore, the number "seven"
always points to a "finished work". And the work of our
redemption is also finished—Christ rests his case for
our justification at the Blood of the Cross; (Jn 19:30) this is
what we call *The Finished Work*, an extremely important
point; for we cannot really know the God of the Bible,
and we cannot properly interpret the Bible unless we
know Love's Finished Work.

The word "pillars" brings to mind an infrastructure
that gives stability and support to a completed system;
"seven pillars" brings to mind a picture of a completed,
enclosed system—i.e. the truth, the whole truth, and
nothing but the truth. "Seven pillars" represents God's
support system for the total, time-space, faith-based,
material universe. Born-again believers are begotten
of the Word of truth, (Ja 1:18) The Spirit of Truth guides

us into all truth, (Jn 16:13) Truth is the person of the Lord Jesus Christ, (Jn 1:1, 14:6) and God's Word is truth. (Jn 17:17)

Wisdom is more than just a word; it is the person of God—the Lord Jesus Christ. (1Co 1:30) God has built a house—a temple of truth—for the Son and His bride, the Church. (Je 33:11; Re 21:9) It is a place where He, and all He is, dwells with us and in us, covering, sheltering, protecting us from the enemies of our soul, and keeping us securely in His love. (Ju 21,24)

The wisdom of God has built His house, and the building material he uses is line upon line, precept upon precept, truth—doctrine inherent in the heart and soul of the believer. (Is 28:10-13; Ps 51:6) This is the same truth that is the building blocks of the entire material universe; it is the essence of the mysterious binding force of the atomic and subatomic nature of all things, seen and unseen. (Co 1:16,17)

Love gives coherence to all of life and existence.

When a believer's heart is dealing with difficulties in life, Wisdom's house is a wonderful place of abiding with Him. (Jn 14:1-6) When the heart is hurting with the pain of loneliness, or despair, or defeat, or guilt, or shame, or fear, Wisdom's house is beautiful for situation—a place of comfort and consolation for a troubled soul. (Ps 48:1-3, 119:50,76) When the heart is worried, or insecure, or anxious, or full of fear, Wisdom's house is a strong tower of safety for the righteous. (Pr 18:10) When the storms of life are raging all around; yea, when death itself stands at the door, this heart knows that its house isn't built upon the sand of the world, it's built upon Truth, the Living Word—The Rock of our salvation, which is Jesus Christ. (Ps 62:1-7, Mt 7:24-27) Love never fails, and neither does Truth!

For we know that if our earthly house, this tent, is destroyed, we have a building from God, a house not made with hands, eternal in the heavens.

2 Corinthians 5:1

This is not "The House That Jack Built"!
This is the house that Wisdom built!
Heaven and earth must pass away,
but this house never will.

3

Faith On Trial

Job lost everything in seven consecutive trials of his faith: his house and all that was in it, all everyone of his family, excepting his wife, who was probably not a believer, or Satan would have surely taken her also. Most of us would not have made it through one trial; Job got hit with seven, one after another. And why God would allow such a test? Could it be that Love for Job just wanted an excuse to bless him—even more than it already had; or was it that God saw that Job was ready for a more intimate relationship with Him? Both is true; God is always looking for a way to bless us; always waiting to be gracious to us, always ready to bring us to a higher level of intimacy with Him.

> Then Job arose, and rent his mantle, and shaved his head, and fell down upon the ground, and worshipped, And said, Naked came I out of my mother's womb, and naked shall I return thither: the Lord gave, and the Lord hath taken away; blessed be the name of the Lord.
>
> Job 1:20-21

Job was not without doctrine, or he could never have maintained such an amazing attitude of meekness through his trials; but was this enough? No, it was not. So far it only dealt with the material things in his life, but the trial soon focused upon the inner, self-life. By the time we get to Chapter 19, poor health, physical pain, and especially Job's personal relationships with his friends, has brought him to the epitome of human despair.

"Have pity on me, my friends, have pity, for the hand of God has struck me. Why do you pursue me as God does? Will you never get enough of my flesh?

Job 19:21-22

But suddenly Job has an amazing revelation from Heaven; his attitude changes from total remorse to enthusiasm and rejoicing; he pauses in the midst of his previous thought, looks up to Heaven as though he hears a voice speaking to him; his face lights up with a smile:

Oh that my words were written! Oh, that they were inscribed in a book! That they were engraved on a rock with an iron pen and lead, forever!

Verse 23-24

Suddenly divine light was sent into Job's mind. A moment ago he was aware that all he had came from God, and would go back to God—that he was but a steward of all God blessed him with. Job was content with that, but now God releases Love; it shines through his heart, floods his mind with revelation, and suddenly he has deeper understanding of truth! Job is excited: "Oh! Write this down! ...Oh! Write this in a book! Engrave it in the rocks, and backfill the words with lead, that what I'm about to say might last forever!"

God heard Job's heart; little did he know that his words were about to actually be immortalized in a way he could never even imagine—written into the Holy Bible—which actually will outlast even rocks and lead [Mt 24:35]—for they are settled forever in Heaven. [Ps 119:89] Job's words are now God's Word:

For I know that my Redeemer lives, and He shall stand at last on the earth; And after my skin is destroyed, this I know, that in my flesh I shall see God, Whom I shall see for myself, and my eyes shall behold, and not another. How my heart yearns within me!

Verse 25-27

When the devil turns up the heat, God always has a plan to turn up the Love! And Wisdom is at work with a labor of Love [1Th 1:3] ...building her house, truth is being revealed, Love is being perfected.

Pr. Tom Schaller:

Whatever Job already possessed was added-to as he received the love of God: a knowing that he was unconditionally loved, that even his weak flesh would return to God in a glorified essence, that he has a Redeemer whose plan and purpose is to restore— not only his material wealth—but the wealth that is his very life and being in Christ. What an awesome revelation to a troubled heart. Oh, that we too might have this revelation in every trial of our faith.

It was a time of great trouble for Job, but Wisdom added an entirely new dimension to his understanding—a beautiful new room to his soul structure. And often this is the way the Lord works in our own lives. Our troubles are *not* intended to destroy us, only to build up our faith and hope in Him, [Je 29:11] with Love, and to bring us into a higher level of intimacy with Him.

> *The greatest trial of our faith*
> *is the greatest stepping-stone*
> *to knowing Love*

3

The Virgin's Lamps

We ought to seize every opportunity to allow Wisdom to have her way in our lives. (Pr 4:5-7) Pastor Carl Stevens, the founder of our ministry, wrote a booklet entitled, *Just Let God Love You.* Every first-time visitor to our Church receives a complementary copy of it. We might say this is the blueprint Wisdom uses in building her house: Just let God love you. If we will learn how to do that one thing, we will be prepared for anything the world, the flesh, or the devil himself can ever bring against us. Yes! Love has that kind of power and much, much more.

Jesus told a parable about ten virgins. (Mt 25:1-23) They were all to be attendants at a wedding procession from the bride's home to a wedding feast the groom had prepared at their home-to-be. The tradition was, when the groom would suddenly come knocking at his bride's door, the virgins' part was to light the way for a procession to the couple's new home with their oil-burning lamps. Now, the Church is pictured as the bride, and we are all virgins, as born-again believers—the light of the world. (Mt 5:14) Our minds are as lamps and the oil is the Spirit of Truth. (Jn 14:17) The unannounced coming of the groom may refer to the rapture of the church (1Co 15:51-54) but it could also refer the hour of death, whenever that may be, for believer or unbeliever.

Five of the ten virgins allowed the oil in their lamps to deplete to a very low level. They all had oil, but five of the ten did not have enough. We could say that five out of ten Christians today are not spiritually prepared for what God wants to do in their lives. In our day-to-day life it's very easy to allow our enemies to rearrange out priorities and take us right out of the perfect will of God. We often become familiar with our calling, neglect the hearing of the Word, or we hear it but neglect the application; all these negatives deplete our reservoir of oil—our sensitivity to the leading of the Holy Spirit, our ability to apply faith in God to details of life, our preparedness for the Lord's service as a vessel of honor [2Co 4:7; 1Th 4:4]

Our spiritual house is not built in a day; it's prepared precept-by-precept, line upon line, [Is 28:10-11] as any material house would be: one brick upon another, one beam hear, and another there, a window, a door, a room, step by step all the way through to completion. And we need to be continuously receiving doctrine for it is the building material; that means hearing and doing God's Word [Ja 1:22] in a program of discipleship. This is the spiritual application of the pillars of truth being hewn out, [Pr 9:1] set in their proper place as integral parts of a completed soul structure.

> Therefore whoever hears these sayings of Mine, and does them, I will liken him to a wise man who built his house on the rock: 1and the rain descended, the floods came, and the winds blew and beat on that house; and it did not fall, for it was founded on the rock.
>
> Matthew 7:24-25

In this scripture the hearer and doer of doctrine is a wise man who builds his house upon the rock; and that rock is Jesus himself, the Rock of Salvation, [2Sa 22:3,47; Ps 18:46] but there's more: It also refers to disciples— those who hear and do Jesus' teaching are as wise men building their house. Wind, rain, and the floods of adversity beat upon this house but it does not fail for it is founded on the rock, and is held together—has unity in the Body of Christ—by Love. This is *Agape's* house, and *Agape* never fails.

But everyone who hears these sayings of Mine, and does not do them, will be like a foolish man who built his house on the sand: and the rain descended, the floods came, and the winds blew and beat on that house; and it fell. And great was its fall.

Verse 26

The day will come—and it may or it may not be the rapture suddenly and unexpectedly the Bridegroom is knocking at the door. He's ready to take us to a higher level of intimacy with Himself; the divinely ordained time for the plan to be put into action has come, and if we have not been a wise builder, we are not prepared. We immediately get on our knees and pray fervently; sometimes our prayers are answered on the spot, but we don't even know it because our faith is weakened by our laxity; our miracle is right under our nose, but we can't see it. The power of the Lord is present to heal, but we don't believe. The darkness of our circumstances blinds us, and we have no oil for our lamps. The Holy Spirit is in us and Love is available but we don't know how to receive it and apply it.

We hurriedly try to borrow oil from others, but they cannot help us; they have barely enough for their own use. We run to the Church, to the Body; we seek counseling in sorrow and tears, we call everybody we know, but all that can really be told us is what we have heard many times over. And we say, "Oh, I know that; you're preaching to the choir! I don't need a sermon; I need help." And it may be that the choir needs some good preaching; in any case, we cannot be comforted. The trouble is, yes, we do know that, but we don't possess it, and it doesn't possess us. We've heard the truth, but we haven't allowed faith to apply it to our experience; we haven't internalized it, we actually have not let God love us. God loved us with perfect love, but we didn't allow His love to be made perfect through us; we heard it but we did not do it. Our foundation is weak because the pillars of truth are not in place. It may be that there is no foundation at all; the entire structure of the soul is only supported by our religious belief, culture, friends, something or someone—all of which is as the sand of the sea if pillars of truth are not securely in place.

This parable is about spiritual *preparedness*: Doctrine, thinking with God in categories of truth—the one thing that equips us for the Christian experience in a world where tribulation is a certainty. (Jn 16:33) Our Christian brothers and sisters—other virgins—would actually be happy to share their oil if only they could, but we can't share preparedness, and we can't get it at Walmart either. Preparedness is as seven pillars of truth; the wise man has hewn them out of a labor of Love, a work of faith, and a patience of hope (1Th 1:3) in the Lord Jesus Christ and his Finished Work.

> *Love never fails*
> *because it is Omnipotent—*
> *having the strength of*
> *Truth.*

3

When Someone Throws Dirt In Your Face

King David's son, Absalom, led a rebellion against his father. He had gathered an army [2 Sa 15] and was on his way to Jerusalem to actually take the throne of Israel by force. David fled with his entire household, including his servants, and his mighty men. [2 Sa 16:6] They were passing through the town of Bahurim when a man called Shimei came along side of them, and began to shout curses and insults, and throw stones and dirt at David.

"Go away, man of blood! You're a worthless nobody! God has avenged the house of Saul, our rightful king, whose blood you shed. He has given your throne to your own son! You brought this shame upon yourself! And you are a blood thirsty, evil man!" shouted Shimei. [2Sa 16:7-8]

Now we read that David's mighty men were at his side during this whole episode. We're not told whether Shimei was brave, or ignorant—perhaps he was a little of both— but he definitely was in serious danger because David's military commanders were not known as his "mighty men" for no good reason. Very capable soldiers they were, and would think nothing at all of taking a life, especially the life of one who threatened or insulted the King they knew and loved, and would willingly die for. One of these men was David's nephew, Abishai, son of Zeruiah, and brother of Joab, David's five-star General of the Army.

Abishai asked, "Why should this stinky, old, dead dog be allowed to curse and insult my Lord the King? Please! I pray thee, my Lord...Please! Give to me the honor of taking his ugly head off!"

Now, Abishai was well able to take Shimei out with a single stroke of his sword, and David was well able to allow him to do so. He could have said, "Yes! Do it,

Abishai! Get this jackass out of my face! Do it slowly; he
needs to learn what its like to suffer as I do."

It is so easy to let a wounded heart do our thinking
for us: "Yes! Kill! Kill!" it will say. "My misery and pain
needs a sacrifice! Kill!"

Pr. Tom Schaller:

Thinking connected with injury is a deadly
combination. My injured emotions say to my mind,
"You have hurt me! You allowed it this happen...I
think about it all the time, and it's very painful."
Blame feeds a hunger for revenge with accusation;
the emotions are quick with it, "It's your fault! How
are you going to make up for all the miserable pain
I go through?"

Gossip, also, fuels the fire of anger; and I may
not initiate the gossip but when someone else does I
enjoy listening to it because it takes the pressure off
my guilt-laden emotions: "Ah ha! I guess I'm not the
only one that goes through things like this! Everybody
is doing it, so it must be OK!"

Not only has David lost the love of a favorite son; he
lost his kingdom also. Not only does his son want his
throne, he wants his life! Many would not blame David
at all if he killed Absalom—even if he is a favorite son.
Few would fault David for anything he did under these
circumstances. And we must also remember that he's
the same man who, as a boy, killed the giant Goliath
with a slingshot. (1Sa 17) David is not intimidated by his
son's ambition. He actually doesn't need Abishai; he
might have easily taken Shimei himself. But David
loves his son and fears hurting him far more than losing
his throne, or even his own life; but David's mind is
operating on a different level.

Could it be that God has arranged a lesson in loving
one's enemies? Could it be that He will use David's heart
after Him—even in the midst of such dire circumstances—

to bring this lesson home to the heart of everyone concerned? We can be sure of is this: God knows David's heart and He is always up to it when it comes to bringing His people into situations intended to teach and promote them. Every trial of our faith is more precious than gold that perishes [1 Pe 1:7-8] because it promotes us in the Kingdom of God, in grace, and in knowledge of Him.

> But the king said, "What have I to do with you, you sons of Zeruiah? So let him curse, because the Lord has said to him, 'Curse David.' Who then shall say, 'Why have you done so?'" And David said to Abishai and all his [David's] servants, "See how my son who came from my own body seeks my life. How much more now may this Benjamite? Let him alone, and let him curse; for so the Lord has ordered him. It may be that the Lord will look on my affliction, and that the Lord will repay me with good for his cursing this day." And as David and his men went along the road, Shimei went along the hillside opposite him and cursed as he went, threw stones at him and kicked up dust.
>
> 2 Samuel 16:10-13

"My Lord, aren't you hurting enough? You don't have to take this! Please; allow me to shut his filthy mouth!" Abishai pleaded.

"Abishai! Joab! Let it go! He's cursing me, not you!" David replied.

David has learned a precious lesson in life because of his affair with Bathsheba [2Sa 11]—to let God Love Him—and he knows *agape's* order of operation is—regardless of how his emotions feel about it—he will let God love him in his circumstances; then he will love God in his circumstances; then he will love himself in his circumstances; then he will love others in his circumstances; even his enemies who created his circumstances; he will Love with the same Love he receives from God. This is precisely what it means to Just Let God Love You.

Then Love connects with truth in the inward parts and out of David's mouth come gracious words that reveal perfected Love:

Sure it hurts! Of course I'm humiliated, but that's OK! It may be that God has told him to curse me. If He did, who are we to question God's plan or purpose? Maybe it's good that Shimei curses me; maybe it's good for me to be humble and broken before Him. If this is God's plan He will sustain me. Let's not deal with these things on the level of our wounded emotions. Let's live in a mind that's bigger than our problems, bigger than our hurt, bigger than our worries and fears; let's live in doctrine, because it is able to build us up in the inner man, and manifest the nature and the reality of Christ in our life.

Listen to me! Everyone! My own flesh and blood seeks my life; why wouldn't Shimei also want to kill me? Yes! I'm hurting, but nothing he can say or do will make the pain any worse than it already is. Let him curse me if it makes him feel better! If this is God's will, it may be that He wants to use this humiliation as an excuse to bless me, and all of you as well; maybe even Shimei himself. Leave him alone! Praise God!

They honored their king's request; David and his men passed by, and Shimei continued along side cursing and throwing stones and dirt at them, but nobody raised a hand to him or resisted him in any way. And I have to believe he was absolutely, totally astonished by that grace and mercy. Can you imagine it; a little commoner like, Shimei facing off with David's mighty men? And I wonder what affect this had upon him. I wonder if this manifestation of Love was the very thing he needed? And would God cause all this fuss just to get Shimei... saved?? Is one soul worth more than the entire planet? What do you think? Would Jesus really leave the 99 to seek the one?

Squillions of marvelous things about Love can only be revealed in the eternity of Heaven, (Is 64:4; 1Co 2:9) and they assuredly will be revealed there; it very well might take forever but it will be revealed.

Pr. Tom Schaller:

We can choose to live in *agape*; we are well able to let *agape* reign in our lives, we do not have to think with self-interest, we can think with the mind of Christ. If people are upset or troubled about one thing or another they don't want our emotional reactions, they don't want our criticism, and they don't want to be questioned about how they got themselves into such a miss. What they actually do want is to be loved with perfected Love.

We don't need to brood over assumed faults, we don't need to think out of personal injury, we don't need to be vengeful or suspicious of the motives of others, and we do not need to live in envy or covetousness. These things are not in our new heart; humility and meekness is there. A mind that is receptive to doctrine is there, and we're occupied with that because it builds us up in the love of God and the most holy faith. (Jude 21,21) When we relate to those who would unjustly accuse us we're able to say, "May the Lord bless them, for they know not what they do. Let's try to work this out in all humility, and go on with an attitude of Love, one for another, because we genuinely are concerned for one another."

We do not need to live with an eye for an eye, or an injury for an injury attitude, because we have a heart quickened with *agape* love for all people. We really do care about people who make mistakes in life. We really do care about those who are often foolish and unwise in decision-making—as anyone can be at times. Men and women are free to live their lives before God as they choose. We respect that freedom, because we think with Love. When we consider those of a faith other than our own, it's never about our difference it's always about our likeness. Love thinks no evil—it never thinks in terms of things we can't agree upon, it thinks in terms of things we do agree upon.

We want to think with God in the construct of divine viewpoint. We want to think with *agape* and doctrine that teaches us about the Body of Christ, the ministry of God, the gifts and calling that are without repentance. (Ro 11:29)

With limited knowledge, why ever would we assume, or presume, or be suspicious, or critical. Our philosophy of life must be derived from a mind filled with doctrine, and a new heart filled with the love of God. When a Shimei comes along side throwing curses, and stones, and dirt—and he always will—we simply say, "Leave him alone. It may be that God will bless me because of this mistake." We pray for Shimei, that he might be encouraged in Love, that he may be edified and corrected, and built up in the Body of Christ, and the person of God...And let it begin with us, Lord, we will receive the Love you want them to have; then we will give it out with joy in our hearts.

If we have this mind we will never fail because Love never fails. Those we Love most may want our heads, and we may find ourselves in the lowest valley of despair—on the run—we may have curses, and stones, and dirt thrown in our face; we may even find ourselves being crucified with Christ, (Ga 2:20) but this one thing we know:

Wisdom has built her house.
She has hewn out seven pillars.
And...
"Everything's Alright In My Father's House".

Chapter 4
— Love Always Wins —

The Model Church—The Link To Love

> Then Peter said to them, "Repent, and let every one of you be baptized in the name of Jesus Christ for the remission of sins; and you shall receive the gift of the Holy Spirit. For the promise is to you and to your children, and to all who are afar off, as many as the Lord our God will call." And with many other words he testified and exhorted them, saying, "Be saved from this perverse generation." Then those who gladly received his word were baptized; and that day about three thousand souls were added to them. And they continued steadfastly in the apostles' doctrine and fellowship, in the breaking of bread, and in prayers.

> Acts 2:38-42

Peter's preaching did a masterful job of bringing the Gospel home to the hearts of a multitude that had gathered in Jerusalem to celebrate the Jewish Passover Feast. A powerful Holy Spirit anointing brought in conviction of sin, and of righteousness, and of judgment; (Jn 16:8) the people gladly received his words and when Peter gave the invitation to receive Jesus Christ as Savior about three thousand souls were added to the Church. And they continued steadfastly in the apostles' doctrine, in fellowship in the Body of Christ, in Communion, and in prayer.

The life of God's family consists of perseverance in:
1. *Salvation*—saving souls by the preaching of the Word. (Verses 38-41)

2. *Fellowship*—a program including:
   (a) *Doctrine*—teaching and application. (Verse 42a)
   (b) *Communion*—remembrance of the Finished Work. (Verse 42b)
   (c) *Prayer*—our Heavenly connection in all the above. (Verse 42c)

Over the years these principles have been the corner stone of our Church and our vision because they minister to the heart of every believer. Every disciple "continued steadfastly" in them (Greek: *ēn proskartereō:* persevered*).* Christian fellowship in the Body of Christ is sure to involve many a trial of faith that will demand pure perseverance.

> *The key to perseverance in the faith is...*
> *our link to Love,*
> *without which we can do nothing.*

4

Come to Love

Who can say, I have made my heart clean, I am pure from my sin?

Proverbs 20:9

Pr. Tom Schaller:

Who can say, "I have made my heart clean, I am pure from my sin?"

Nobody can! There is great misconception about how "good" we are, and its common in many, many people.

No matter how hard we try, it simply is not in the heart of fallen mankind to lift himself up to God's standard of holiness. (Je 17:9; Ro 3:23; 5:12, 6:23) What we need is a new heart! Without a Savior I am absolutely without God and without hope in this present world. (Ep 2:12) Christ in me is my only hope of glory; (Co 1:27) through him—the Blood of his Cross—I come to the Father (Jn 14:6) and actually receive a new heart and a new spirit—a totally new, spiritual, frame of reference for my sorry, sorry soul. (Ez 11:17-20, 18:31, 36:26) But now I have a hunger for doctrine because this new heart has an insatiable appetite for truth.

What brought about such an amazing change of attitude in the first Disciples? Were they somehow miraculously changed from desperately wicked and deceitful (Je 17:9) men, to pure and sinless people? Yes and no. Yes, in the sense that they received a new heart and became a literal new creation (2Co 5:17) the instant they received Christ as their Savior. [Definitely a miracle of grace!] But no, in the sense that the old heart is still present in them—as wicked as ever it was—but now it has serious competition because the new heart is the throne room of the King of Kings. (Re 19:16) By His grace they would learn to walk in the Spirit, (Ti 2:11-12, Ga 5:16, 25) in the newness of life, (Ro 6:4) and keep themselves in Love. (Ju 1:21)

The Book-of-Acts Church has all the elements of a perfect Church: leadership, soul-winning, disciples with new hearts quickened by the Holy Spirit, filled with Love, and having a great hunger for doctrine, fellowship, communion, and prayer.

Doctrine gives us the ability to think with God in categories of truth. When we have doctrine in our heart, love can express itself with the mind of Christ; this nurtures fellowship in the Body of Christ, communion with God, and prayer in the Holy Spirit. These four things are essential to the life of the Body. When they're in place we soon see the results: Disciples are in awe of the work of God in the midst of them as many signs and wonders were manifested through the Apostles; they sold their possessions and goods, and gladly shared what they had with one another according to every man's need; they were daily in one accord worshipping God, breaking bread from house to house, eating their meat with gladness and singleness of heart; and they were...praising God, soul winning, and having favor with all the people... (Ac 2:43-47)

The manifestation of Love
automatically
praises Him.

Praise the Lord! Praise God in His sanctuary; Praise Him in His mighty firmament! Praise Him for His mighty acts; Praise Him according to His excellent greatness! Praise Him with the sound of the trumpet; Praise Him with the lute and harp! Praise Him with the timbrel and dance; Praise Him with stringed instruments and flutes! Praise Him with loud cymbals; Praise Him with clashing cymbals! Let everything that has breath praise the Lord. Praise the Lord!

Psalm 150:1-6

David uses the word "praise" no less than thirteen times in this short Psalm. It is also the *last* Psalm, emphasizing the importance of its subject matter. David also says: I will bless the Lord at all times; His praise shall continually be in my mouth. (Ps 34:1)

Why is praise so important? What exactly is "praise"? It is in no way a construct of any human aspiration; it is simply a faith response to initiations of His love. Praise has a miraculous, mysterious way of touching hearts with agape love, and that is precisely what makes it so important to God.

A visiting Pastor from our affiliated church in Azerbaijan recently gave a testimony at one of our services. He told of how, when he was of the Muslim faith, he met some of our missionaries on the streets of his hometown. They invited him to one of their services. He accepted the invitation (as was the Muslim custom if he really did enjoy their company) and he did attend. He shared with us about how he didn't understand any part of the service or the message, and really wasn't even interested. He was only trying to impress his friends with his religious demeanor...but there was something he was very strongly attracted to. He couldn't explain it but it was so powerful that he could not wait to get to the next meeting. He continued to come out to every service and it wasn't long before he was actually enjoying it...and was even participating! He soon became very

105

interested in the Bible, and steadfastly continued in the doctrine of the apostles. Today he's one of our most gifted pastors; we are thoroughly blessed by his portion and fellowship.

But what was it that got his attention and held it? I'm sure there were many things, but I believe it was—in a word—our praises to God; the faith response of the Body of Christ to God's initiations of Love, which came through doctrine, fellowship, communion, and prayer. These elements overflow into the world—as they did immediately after Pentecost in Jerusalem; rivers of living water flowed from our praises—And the Lord added to the church daily...such as would be saved. (Ac 2:47a)

A Church may have many functions but the bottom line of every Church ought to be: ...such as would be saved. At the end of the day the work of the ministry is a labor of Love, a call to take the Gospel of Jesus Christ to the entire world, because God's heart is for the saving of lost souls—He is not willing that any should perish. (Jn 3:16; 2Pe 3:9)

Love is
the fruit of the Spirit.
Praise is
the tree the fruit grows on.

4

Experiencing Agape

Many think Love is a feeling, that's true if its human love only. Human love originates in the emotions, which respond with feelings to initiations of every form of love; this is God's design. But *agape* love thinks, (1Co 13:5) which is something human love cannot do. *Agape* originates in the heart of God, and is shed abroad in and through the new heart of every believer. (Ro 5:5) This truth adds an entirely new dimension to the concept of love. If the operation of the love of God working in and through us is actively thinking, it must be thinking with God in categories of truth—categorical doctrine. This is why the model Church persevered in the doctrine of the Apostles (God's Word taught by the Apostles, systematically and categorically); they were continually experiencing the mind of God thinking thoughts of love toward them. (Je 31:3, 29:11)

If you've ever been in love with someone (and who hasn't?) then you know what its like to have that certain loved one in your thoughts continually, to discover some way to bless them, to cover and protect them, to make them happy, and encourage them to respond to your love.

I remember it well: I was very young and I had my eye on a pretty young lady. I would just sit and scheme and dream all the day long of some way to get her to notice me and respond. Then one day she moved away to another city and that was the end of that. I was heartbroken; O yeah...but it wasn't very long before another pretty young lady came along and I was up to it again. This is human love at its best. My Grandma used to call it "puppy love". But with God there's no such thing! God is seriously in love with every person He ever created, and He's very good at getting our attention, and getting us to respond. But His love is like all His thoughts and ways—as the heavens are higher than the earth, (Is 55:8-9) they are more in number than the sand of the sea (Ps 139:18)—compared to human love. This is divine love...always at its best!

When we're thinking with God we're thinking from a new heart, and the mind is enlightened because it's experiencing true love; submitting to it, rejoicing in it, and always allowing it to work in us to will and do His good pleasure. (Pi 2:13)

> *If the Church is thinking with God,*
> *it is certain to be experiencing Love.*

Pr. Tom Schaller:

Love's channel to the mind is the heart. Through a window to our soul, the heart transmits spiritual light into the mind. But if that window is darkened, covered with sticky, thick, black mud—i.e. the old heart—then the mind sits in darkness and the shadow of death. (Ps 107:10-14)

This is actually the amazing dilemma we face from the moment we're born—we are blind from birth, we might say—spiritually speaking, (Ps 58:13, Ep 4:18) because our old heart is darkened with the stain of Adam's sin. But when we accept Jesus Christ as our Savior, God instantly gives us a new heart—one with crystal clear windows of grace and Finished Work. He didn't just wash the windows He replaced the house! And that's why we love the Bible so much; the new heart craves its teaching—has an empathy for divine love and spiritual light—the Word, truth, doctrine; in this light we see life from an entirely new perspective; this is a wonderful, beautiful thing!

> For with thee is the fountain of life; and in thy light we shall see light.
>
> Psalm 36:9

I still have a vivid recollection of the first few weeks after being born-again. (Jn 3:5) Almost immediately I began to see everything and everyone in a new light. And I couldn't explain it, all I could do is experience it and rejoice. Everything I heard, everything I read, everything I saw, everyone I met, everywhere I went; somehow life just was not the same and it never has been since that first day. It was a good feeling! I didn't understand it, couldn't explain it, but I didn't care; I just loved it. I now know it was the literal light of the love of God, using whatever true knowledge of Him was available, to illuminate my mind, renew it, renovate it, and cleanse it. It was my first—but by no means my last—unforgettable, experience of Love!

The Word of Truth in the mind, enlightened by the glory of Love in the new heart is our venue for abiding with Him. (Jn 15:4-7)

Here is a room exactly as He would have it; every color, every furnishing, every detail of décor is perfect. A crystal skylight is the window of the new heart; and radiating through it are streams of glory that give light and warmth to every corner. But there are no shadows; colors are incredible; the light and warmth of Love seems to come from everywhere...like His glory. Here Jesus and I meet and talk about all the things we admire in one another, testimonies, victories we have won together, times we shared on Planet Earth—waking by faith, together in the garden and gathering the lilies of resurrection life—things past, things present, and things to come; just basking in the *agape* experience of faith, hope, and Love; (1Co 13:13) thoroughly appreciating each other's presence. I love this room!

> My meditation of him shall be sweet: I will be glad in the Lord.
>
> Psalm 104:34

As the Word of God began to be clear in my mind, things I never understood in the Bible were suddenly crystal clear. I began to really read the Word, and everything else I could find that would help me to learn of Him. It wasn't very long at all; God led me to a local church, a pastor-teacher with the Word of grace I needed, (Ac 14:3, 20:32) and a fellowship with plenty of outreaches and a vision for the lost. I continued steadfastly in *doctrine*, in *fellowship*, in *communion*, and in *prayer*. And I absolutely did grow in grace and in knowledge of Love. (2Pe 3:18)

As I write this book nearly thirty years later, my mind is illuminated over and over again with doctrines of Love in many different categories, and I'm still, always and ever, astonished by fresh revelation from Heaven. This is the way it was meant to be; this is the way it is from the moment we're saved by grace through faith (Ep 2:8) until we see him face to face. (1Co 13:12)

Pr. Tom Schaller:

When we have a mind steeped in doctrine we also have sweet fellowship in the Body of Christ! We don't need the world because we have the Lord, His Word, and one another. We're not conformed to the ways of a world as we once were; we're transformed by a mind constantly being renewed and enlightened with doctrine. (Ro 12:1-2) When the Word of God is being preached we get excited regardless of whom the preacher happens to be! We all have fond memories of many hours of fellowship in the Word at services, in classrooms, rap-sessions with the Body, outreach to neighboring cities, mission conferences, and personal time with one another. There are always many ...oooo's, ...aaaah's, and ...wooooow's ...all around us as doctrine shines through our hearts and enlightens every dark corner of the mind; or when someone receives Jesus Christ as their Savior, or gets baptized.

Persevering in doctrine.
fellowship,
communion,
and prayer,
is easy... if I'm having an agape experience.

4

On The Road To Emmaus

There were two very disillusioned disciples walking into the setting sun, down the dusty road from Jerusalem to Emmaus. (Lu 24:13-31) They were so dejected by the loss of the One they had set their hopes upon—the long promised Messiah/Deliverer—that their eyes were totally blinded to the reality of Christ casually strolling along with them. But we know that it is often not easy to see him through tear-filled eyes; he comes to us anyway but often it's in some very discreet way.

The news of Jesus' resurrection could have greatly encouraged them, but it caused even more stress for fear of how the Jews might react when they heard about the "empty tomb". So it is that ignorance and unbelief covers the heart's window on the soul with the black mud of fear, darkness, and sadness that refuses the light of Love. (Lu 1:79)

Jesus admonished them saying, "O foolish ones, and slow of heart to believe everything that the prophets have spoken!" (Lu 24:25)

If there's one serious mistake we all make it's in not believing all of God's Word, for it is our daily bread, (Mt 6:11) a lamp unto our feet, and a light unto our path. (Ps 119:105) Nothing in life is more important than getting to know the God of the Bible, (Php 3:8) and that absolutely begins with believing everything the prophets have spoken.

I wish it were not so, but experience has taught us well that multitudes in the world are very much like these disciples; strolling down life's highway, into the setting sun of life on earth, on their way to Wherever;

unbelieving, discouraged, and very depressed over all sorts of current events and life's details.

The disciples have been foolish, but the resurrected, living, Lord Jesus Christ comes to them anyway, and walks with them, and they experience His love—just soaking it up. Grace is "window washing"; *agape* is shining through, and he is teaching them the Bible—from Moses through Malachi—everything that refers to him. (Lu 24:27) And it doesn't matter that they don't recognize him; his first priority is to enlighten them with doctrine. Doctrine in the mind enables the heart to think with God. It is the agency of the manifestation of Love that heals the brokenhearted, delivers the captives, restores the sight of the blind, and liberates them that are bruised. (Lu 4:18)

As they drew near the village and the place where they would spend the night, they still didn't know it was Jesus who walked with them. But they invited him to stay with them and continue their fellowship; he accepted their invitation. Then, as they sat at supper, he broke bread and offered it to them. And we're not told how it happened—some theologians believe they saw the nail scars in his hands when he offered the bread—but suddenly they recognized Him, and immediately he vanished before their eyes. After all this time with him, how is it that *now* they recognize him? What happened that suddenly revealed him to them? The answers to these questions teach us a key thing that relates to *agape* love:

> *The love of God,*
> *and the Word of God,*
> *reveals the Person of God.*

He didn't personally reveal himself; this had actually already been done—in many dramatic, wondrous ways...numerous times—and they did not get it! Why? What was missing? Love and Doctrine! They haven't believed the Bible! They're called "disciples" but they're unbelieving disciples. Is that possible; to be a disciple and not even be born-again? Oh, yes, just like Judas Iscariot was! Were these disciples born-again? I don't think so. I think this is the primary reason for their blindness. Until I was born again, I wouldn't know the Lord Jesus Christ from my Uncle Joe. And if someone happened along and told me he was Jesus, I'd think he was just another a nut-cake...really! —And after I saw him crucified with my own eyes...absolutely! Jesus makes no attempt to reveal himself to them; he simply Loves them, and teaches them doctrine. When the person of Jesus Christ comes to you and Loves you, you will surely experience that love in spite of yourself and what you know—or what you don't know—about Him. And when he teaches doctrine, he does so with authority; (Mt 7:29) you will know it and it will sink in. (Jn 16:8)

But, once we're saved, he often vanishes. And it's not very long before we're more aware than ever that we are sinners, that we are still spiritually blind at times, that the world is just as real as ever it was before, and—last but by no means least—that the devil never gives up. We thought Christian life would be Heaven on earth, but it just is not so. What is absolutely guaranteed is this: a walk of faith...all the way to the "Pearly Gates" of eternity.

Jesus vanishes right before our eyes, but Love does not; it abides in us forever and our hearts burn within us for more doctrine. (Lu 24:32) We begin to think with the mind of Christ, and Love is released to do what Love does: save us by grace through faith (Ep 2:8-9)—deliver us from spiritual blindness—and constrain our hearts to share the Gospel of Love with all the world. (2Co 5:14) These disciples could get to Jerusalem to tell the others fast enough; they ran all the way. (Lu 24:32-33) And I remember well how I knew I had met the Lord, and I had no idea how to go about it, but my heart did burn within me to tell the world the whole story. And, by the way, that was before I ever had one day of discipleship or Bible College. God does not waste one microsecond; He gives us the desire of our new heart the instant we're saved, (Ps 37:4) and the first and foremost desire is a hunger for the Word—to hear it, and do it, and share and share it, and share it, and share it en ad infinitum!!

Before salvation I had little to say—though I probably talked way too much; but after salvation?? now I cannot stop telling people about Love...and I speak with authority because Love does burn within me, and Love absolutely is the heart of Almighty God.

The setting sun on the dusty road to Emmaus turned into the dawn of a brand new day in the hearts of these precious, discouraged disciples. So it ever is whenever we experience Love.

JOY is...
the experience of L o v e.

4

Evil Thinking

I happened to be a visitor at a church in Sturbridge, MA, recently, and I heard this account of a college professor's philosophy class:

A university professor challenged his class with this question: "Did God create everything that exists?"

"Yes, he did." a student quickly answered.

"God created everything?" the professor asked again.

"Yes, Sir." the student replied, and added "Everything and everyone!"

"If God created everything, then God created evil, since does evil exist. And according to the principle that our works define whom we are, then God is evil." declared the professor. The student became quiet. The professor was thinking he had proven once again that faith in God is only mythological. But another student raised his hand and said, "May I ask a question, Professor?"

"Of course you may!"

The student stood up and asked, "Professor, does cold exist?"

"What kind of question is that? Of course it exists. Have you never been cold?" the professor replied.

"In fact, sir, cold does not exist. According to the laws of physics, what we consider cold is actually only the absence of heat. Every body or object is susceptible to study only if it has or transmits energy. Absolute zero (-460 degrees F) is the total absence of heat. All matter becomes inert and incapable of reaction at that temperature—which, of course, we know can only be theoretically attained—therefore, cold does not exist. We've created this word only to describe how we feel if we don't have enough heat. And I have another question if I may, Professor? Does darkness exist?"

The professor responded, "Of course it does, would you like me to turn of the lights to prove it to you?"

The student replied, "Respectfully, Professor, but once again you are wrong, Sir. Darkness also does not exist. Darkness is only the absence of light. We can study light, but not darkness. In fact, we can use Newton's prism to break light into many colors, and study the various wavelengths of each. But we cannot measure darkness. A simple ray of light can break upon a world of darkness and illuminate it. How can we know how dark a certain space is? We can only measure the amount of light present. Darkness is actually only a term we use to describe what happens when there is no light present." Then, the young man asked, "Sir, does evil exist?"

Now uncertain, the professor responded, "I have already said, evil is evident in the daily example of man's inhumanity to man. It is evident in the multitude of crime and violence we see everywhere in the world. These manifestations are nothing else but evil. Yes, evil definitely does exist!"

To this the student replied, "Evil does not exist, Sir! Or at least it does not exist in and of itself. Evil is actually the absence of God. It is just like darkness or cold—a word used to describe the absence of something else that is real; in this case, God Himself. God did not create evil, and it is not like faith or love, which exist just as light and heat does. Evil is the result of what happens when a human being doesn't have God's love in the heart. It's like the cold that comes when there is no heat, or the darkness that comes when there is no light."

We were not told how the professor graded this student who was very knowledgeable about "evil", but I'm sure he got at least an A++ on this report from God. As soon as I heard it (and it may or not be a true life experience), I knew it was an answer to prayer, because

I actually had been seeking the right words to describe evil thinking for some time, and I could not find the words. And I believe God called me all the way up to Sturbridge, MA, from Baltimore, MD, to hear this report because it illustrates exactly what He wanted me to write—how and why it exists. To me, this was clearly an answer to prayer; I was encouraged and praised God all the way back to Baltimore for His faithfulness. It is such a blessing when we see Love in action; it is always very edifying to us, and it really teaches us to look for Him in every detail of day-to-day life.

If the heart is void of Love, the mind will always default to evil thinking. If I'm unsaved—or even if I'm saved but carnal—when the old heart accesses my mind it finds only darkness and is inclined to think in terms of personal injury. Emotions can easily dominate a dark mind. If there's any light at all, it isn't clear; there's only blindness and insecurity; thoughts of *agape* are actually impossible because the heart defaults to an evil attitude, and the mind thinks evil continuously. I may even have a vision for a ministry, but if I'm thinking evil thoughts, my personal injury is more focused than any vision; my emotions are more intense than any other reasoning, and they're always going to be my first priority. Truth will "take a backseat" every time—and that is incredible—if I brood over assumed thoughts of others (which may not even be real) and magnify the faults of other's (real or imputed). This is Evil thinking, not Love thinking.

Suspicious thinking is also evil, and it comes from the darkened mind of the old heart; so does thinking enviously, or unjustly with opinions that correspond with my feelings only. I've seen it all to often in my own heart concerning someone thousands of miles away. When I think of them I'm suspicious, questioning, wondering about them, imagining that they're scheming to hurt me in some way. But I know this is coming from my old heart, thinking outside of divine love, without a doctrinal frame of reference—vain imaginations (Ro 1:21 2Co 10:5)—so I purpose to let Love in and cast evil thoughts out.

Jesus came into this world with all the weakness and limitation of any human being, except that he was born of the virgin, by the power of the Holy Spirit (not a human father). He was, therefore, born without a sin nature; therefore, as he lived his life in this world, spiritual light was constantly flooding his mind. Of course he was also God, but he lived here among us as a man; and he increased in wisdom and stature. (Lu 2:52)

When he was with his disciples he was always ministering to them, touching their hearts with Love, investing in them, and believing in them. He wasn't living in suspicion, or wounded emotions, or brooding upon their faults—which were many. He had no personal injury troubling him, or working on his emotions in any way; he lived in absolute Love. Love would just look at these men, and they would know they were Loved. He corrected them, challenged them in the faith, and even put their feet to the fire occasionally; but they knew he was different, they knew he loved them with Love, which they had never before experienced, that he never one time thought any evil whatsoever of any one of them. And they were irresistibly drawn to his fellowship...by Love.

Pr. Tom Schaller:

When we believe, God brings light into our mind, and we begin to live and think with love by faith. We begin to think with God, and believe that life in Him is awesome, because with Love all things are possible.

Love never fails—or we can turn it around and say...Love Always Wins!

If Jesus would, in some miraculous way, appear to you today—face to face—and you were to look into his eyes, He would communicate His love right into your heart, and that love would be extremely powerful in affecting the person you are. It would melt your heart like butter and you would know that this love would never fail you. You would know He is for you, you would know He is enduring all things, hoping all things, and believing all things about you, without ever being suspicious of you, or envious of you, or thinking of you in any evil context whatsoever. You would experience His love; it would affect you, it would heal you, and you would know that you are loved as you have never been loved before. You would know that, even if you would forsake Him, He would go right on loving you, just as he did Peter and the others, and He would never, not for one second, not for any reason, ever leave you or forsake you. You would know that! He would just look into your eyes and say: "I love you! I'll never let you down. You can't lose when you have me as your God. You're more than a conqueror through me who has loved you from eternity, chosen you, and called you out of darkness into the glorious light of my love. You're a winner! You cannot lose! And wild horses couldn't drag me away for you.

His love for you is always going to make you... A W I N N E R !

Consider and meditate upon the great truth of His love in us, filling our hearts, ministering to us, and others through us! This is a profound, powerful, awesome thing! Then consider that we can know by faith—with a certainty—that all our relationships are based upon His love; not frivolous, self-seeking, sentimental, wistful human love, but upon perfect, unconditional, unfailing, eternal Love! What a difference real love makes!

All my life I've had to struggle to maintain a front because I was insecure around people and wanted to be confident, in control, and self-sufficient; I considered anything less to be sheer weakness. There's nothing more stressful in life than trying to be someone you're not, or someone everybody thinks you are, but you just know you are not. But now I do know this: I am what I am by the grace of God, (1Co 15:10) and I'm confident that the Body of Christ is content with that because I know we think no evil of one another in His love. This great truth sets me free indeed. (Jn 8:36)

Pr. Tom Schaller:

We can hardly believe how great and wonderful this is. We have to make a conscious effort to fully realize what it means to Love and to be Loved by people who think with Love. This is amazingly reassuring, edifying, and comforting to know: Someone is looking at me, not seeing me in the context of their personal injury, or something they imagine about me, or suspicion, or assuming in any way...They're knowing I have a real fault yet, not knowing me on the basis of that fault, they see me and my fault in the context of God's love, and they Love me, and that alone makes me a winner every time.

Peter denied the Lord three times in the hour of His greatest need. Then, to make matters worse, he left Jesus' calling—to fish for men—and went fishing for fish, and took most of the other Disciples with him. Now, I would think that they all were in line for some kind of serious chastisement—especially Peter. After all Jesus had done for them it would be easy for him to think that way. But if we know Jesus' heart we're sure that it is only thinking one thing: Love.

In John 21:15-19, Jesus speaks to Peter in particular and the Disciples in general with that look of Love in his eye:

Feed my sheep, Peter. I know you're hurting, and I do care about that; I'm for you! I love you with perfect love regardless of how you love me. Just feed my sheep, Peter, and as you do, the flow of my love through you will heal you're hurting heart and it will heal other hearts as well.

When you were young you girded yourself and went wherever you wanted, but when you're older, another will gird you, and take you where you would never go—even to the Cross you denied three times, Peter—and there you will experience my love, as never before. Human love will put you in a box, but my love will launch you out of the box, and into a vision; it will set you free, and you will be free indeed. (Jn 8:32, 36)

"Feed my sheep" is the doorway:
Perfect love comes in,
Perfected Love goes out.

4

The Eurocon Experience

Pr. Tom Schaller:

The Israelites in the wilderness would say, "Where's the food, God? I know! You brought us out here in the desert because there weren't enough graves in Egypt; is that it?? You want us to starve, God. By the way, where's the water, God? Are you just going to let us die of thirst? ...My kids are dying, God!! ... Egypt was a paradise compared to this."

We have to wonder at the audacity of these primitive believers. They saw many amazing miracles, but they soon became familiar and began to see God as something of a "sugar daddy". But it's much easier to be like them than we can imagine. I'll be the first to admit that I sometimes fail in this area myself; knowing the Word—but not really—because when the pressure is on I don't live in it. If I did I wouldn't react the way I do. Sometimes I just lack wisdom, and sometimes, having wisdom, I lack understanding and make bad decisions in spite of myself. I've been in my flesh enough to know that I do not want it to dominate my thought life. When it does, I become like an Israelite in the wilderness. I don't want my old heart of unbelief to put its finger in God's face.

I want to have the courage of faith to take responsibility for my failure, confess my sin and say: "Forgive me, Father; fill me afresh with your Spirit. Show me the sin of my heart and let the light of your love illuminate my mind. I know that it's only by the power of perfect love that my heart will think no evil. I receive your love in all humility; it is the desire of my heart, Lord. I know that without Love I'm a loser, but I know that I really do have it, and that automatically makes me a winner. Amen!"

We had one of the largest crowds ever at our Budapest Eurocon. It was a precious time of fellowship in the Body. On one occasion, as we were just standing around after a service, a Brother from Austria said, I thought it was all over; I had given up! I thought I could never find a church where I could just sit there and receive the Word, and have the peace and presence of God just wash over me, and cleanse me. This fellowship is a great blessing to me. And we would say, "Yes! We know it's true! We're surprised also!" But we shouldn't be. This is what continuing steadfastly—persevering—in the doctrine of the Apostles always does. We're so blessed by Love and doctrine that it's almost too good to be true. And we're not producing our joy by any human effort; it's the very nature of God and His people, and our fellowship—God's channel of charity. It's Love that thinks no evil. It is definitely not a construct of a mind derived from a heart filled with evil where we actually challenge God—even put our finger in His face and say, "Not good—You didn't do it! You hurt me! Not good—You failed me!"

No! That's a loser talking, not a winner!

*Love always wins,
because it thinks no evil of anyone;
not even a "loser".*

4

Deliverance

> And they steadfastly persevered, devoting themselves
> constantly to the instruction and fellowship of the
> apostles, to the breaking of bread [including the Lord's
> Supper] and prayers.
>
> Acts 2:42 (Amplified)

I've know believers who truly want to be delivered from one form of bondage or another—sometimes many forms—but they refuse to steadfastly persevere in the Word, and they're definitely not delivered. Jesus' Disciples needed deliverance, even after Pentecost and signs and wonders in their midst. They were devoted, meaning they were given over to display, study, and open discussion and instruction in doctrine; they were assimilating, absorbing, and integrating truth into their mind in a way that affected their very personalities. They were being changed, conformed to the image of Christ. What an awesome difference this makes compared to being conformed to the world. They were continually persevering, meaning they were at it all the time— sometimes for a long period of time—not because they had to be, but because their hearts loved it and burned with a desire for it. This is not by human design; it is simply the nature of the new heart. What a marvelous, wonderful, precious gift of God it is, to have to have a brand new heart filled with love that thrives upon truth that sets us free. No form of bondage, no bad habit, no guilt trip, no demonic stronghold, no idiosyncrasy, no evil the devil can devise, can conquer Love.

Pr. Tom Schaller:

I rejoice whenever I see the Body being faithful to come out to services, because I want so much for them to reap all the rewards of fellowship in the Word of truth that abounds when we assemble in His name. We never know when, but healings do happen; deliverances happen often; some we hear about, but I know there are many of a confidential nature that we never do. On a given day, a certain word is given under a certain anointing and the plan of God is for a certain person to be there. They are and it happens: Healing! Deliverance! Miracles! Salvations! Anything is possible! God is always watching and waiting to be gracious, (Is 30:18) because He wants His people to be winners.

I'm totally blessed whenever I consider how effectively God uses the Body to edify those that desperately need Love, or understanding, or a word of encouragement, or a prayer, or sometimes just a smile, or a friendly handshake. A labor of Love abounds in our midst as we're gathering together, eating together, hearing His Word together, believing together, seeing one another's face, hearing one another's portion, praying for one another, bearing one another's burdens; all these things and many more, edify us with amazing Love.

> As iron sharpens iron, so a man sharpens the countenance of his friend.
>
> Proverbs 27:17

Sometimes just a certain look, in the eye of a certain person, is used of God to communicate a word of wisdom that will sharpen spiritual skills like nothing else can. And sometimes it's painful to be sharpened; there is a faith factor in fellowship that demands continually, steadfastly persevering in fellowship.

> As in water face reflects face, so a man's heart reveals the man.
>
> Proverbs 27:19

The water of the Word is like a mirror. As we look into it and consider Body-life application we see one another's reflections. I might just look at you and suddenly the Holy Spirit will recall a scripture to my mind. Sometimes I look at a Pastor, and God speaks to me saying, "Do you see the heart of my servant here? This is what I mean by the "unfeigned love of the brethren." (1Pe 1:22) And immediately my heart is challenged by his example. I cannot tell you how many times over the years the example of a Pastor's heart before my very eyes has been used of God to change my life.

Fellowship in the Body of Christ is a precious gift that flourishes in God's love, and delivers us from a multitude of sin. (1Pe 4:8)

Pr. Tom Schaller:

I encourage all read these words to go to God with a this prayer of faith:

Lord, I want to be lighthearted, to rejoice in your love. There's so much trouble in the world, but I don't want to be negative or heavy. I want to share your burden for the lost, to have a new heart overflowing with your love, and your mind. This is the way, and I will walk in it continuing steadfastly in the doctrine of the apostles.

Some have set a course leading to absolute destruction, and I want to be used by you to save them from it. Is there a way I could care more, Lord? Is there is a way I could minister to some hurting soul, help them to bear a heavy burden? Could I be an evangelist, or a preacher, or a pastor, or a missionary? I want to be serious about my calling. I want to learn how to come to you in prayer, how to be used by you to share the Gospel with others; how to be able to say to someone, "Could I show you in the Bible where it says you can be born again?" "Could I bring you to my Church where you might hear a really good message about love?"

I want to be in the midst of people who are serious about God and life, yet who have the joy of the Lord in all they say and do. I want to be with people who are serious about their mission in life, and yet happy and joyful in the Lord. I want to have fellowship with people who even put their hard earned money in the offering basket. I want to serve you with the kind of people who will have an all night, prayer meeting on a mountaintop, (Lu 6:12) and then come down and call their disciples together to spend time with them— invest in them. I want to serve you with people who make disciples, teach them how to love one another, always believing the best for them, investing in their teenagers, having hope and encouragement, thinking no evil, enduring all things, believing all things, bearing all things, and hoping all things. These people are the testimony of Christ in a dark world. They break the bread of communion, and continue steadfastly in fellowship. This is the kind of people I know I need to be with, Lord. Please lead me into this kind of fellowship.

Lead me into a season of prayer, Lord. There are principalities and powers that challenge your kingdom on earth, but we can move them. We can bind them and they'll be bound!

Lord, raise people up who are useful in ministry and the work of faith; even the person with the smallest faith, barely holding on, can be filled with hope and encouragement. Lord, give me a burden in the depths of my heart for people who are perishing— the soul that is the very closest to the reality of hell.

In Jesus' Name; Amen!"

4

Words Of Encouragement To The Saved

The Lord Jesus Christ sends us into the world as the Father sent him; (Jn 20.21) to bring the message of Love to the lost, to see people be born-again, saved, washed clean in the blood of the Lamb, have a new heart, fellowship in the Body of Christ, and have their minds renewed.

Pr. Tom Schaller:

Be very careful about what you read in the privacy of your homes. Why read wicked, evil, fleshly, carnal garbage that feeds your old heart? Why not imbibe in the Bible, doctrine, and theology? Why not read the Word of God, think about it, meditate upon it, walk in it, and watch the light of the Lord come into our mind. You will see with crystal clarity that God is in our midst. I know, this is the way it is right now, but it's our prayer more than ever before, that in our testing we won't be found out there in La-La Land with the old heart and a mind that thinks evil continually. We want to be in the Spirit, going about our Father's business, making disciples, teaching them, going into the highways and hedges, going to a Zacchaeus out on a limb, a Nicodemus in the dark of night, a woman at a well—all the while knowing His love has done it all.

Draw near with a pure heart, be washed with the water of the Word, enlightened by the Apostles doctrine, encouraged by the fellowship of the saints, edified in the breaking of bread, and delivered by the power of prayer. Do not withdraw; draw near! The Lord will build you up in His most Holy Faith, and keep you in His love, (Jude 20,21) and you will begin to know and believe that love always wins.

We open our mouths and speak boldly as we ought to. And we speak lovingly, in the class rooms, at the water fountains, in the restaurants, on the streets, pleading as the Lord himself would plead; not willing that any should perish, but that all should come to repentance. (2Pe 3:9)

We plead with the Love of the Lord:

Please listen! Please! I know you have problems; I have them too but I also have a Savior, a new heart constrained by His love, and a renewed mind that doesn't ever think evil. Neither does it ever say its God's fault! It says, my God is so good, my God is Gracious, my God is merciful, my God is awesome, and my God is Love.

So we get together, and we go to the Bible and read! And someone has a psalm, someone a verse, a prophecy, a word in season, a song, a beautiful heart; someone has a countenance, shining, loving people with the love of the Lord. This is what Jesus came to us with, and this is what he left his Disciples. When the people saw it in Acts 2, they knew this was real love and they wanted it. That's how it should always be! That's how it is with us who believe. And when the world sees us it sees that there is something different, because God has set a difference between the world and us. (Ex 11:17) The way we talk, how we think, how we love, is not the way of the world.

> *If we have no Love*
> *for the lost*
> *it's because we're not hearing*
> *His calling.*

4

Words of Warning To The Unsaved

Pr. Tom Schaller:

We live in perilous times! [(2Ti 3:1-7)] I'm very saddened by what I see in people's lives in the world today. They experience much suffering because they simply don't know what God has for them. Evil hearts just cannot believe that God is God, the Bible is the Bible, the Body is the Body, the Holy Spirit is the Holy Spirit, and Heaven is Heaven...and I shudder to think that hell is hell! These great truths are absolute, but the world, the flesh, and the devil would make them to be abstract, relative, and flexible.

We live in a small world in these last days; I call it a *global society*. With all our cultural and ethnic differences we really are all very much alike when it comes to basic wants and needs, and even likes and dislikes. I believe that the work Satan schemed and began back in the Garden, took into account the coming of this present age. He had a plan from the very beginning that is just now coming to fruition. Down through the ages he has been systematically building upon a diabolical venue to deceive the entire world into living by a *pseudo faith*. This is deadly because it's diametrically opposed to divine design.

The totality of the material universe by God's sovereign ordination exists as a faith economy. The Bible tells us:

Without faith it is impossible to please Him. [(He 11:6)]
The just shall live by faith. [(Ro 1:17, Ga 3:11, He 10:38)]

> We're saved by grace through faith. (Ep 2:8)
> Whatsoever is not of faith is sin. (Ro 14:23)

For millennia Satan has been seeding every social discipline—art, music, science, medicine, literature, psychology, philosophy, theology, etc.—with lies and deception, relativism, abstractism, and humanism, all of which compromise absolutes. The result of this is a global society that has an aversion to absolutes; this is the very essence of existentialism—a leap-of-faith mentality that seems to be faith but is actually *dead* faith—not a living faith that reveals Love. The existentialist is so deceived that he usually doesn't even know he is one; and if he does, he cannot really define his philosophy because he lacks the necessary absolutes. I call existentialism *the culmination of the corrupted wisdom of the ages*—the end product of a multitude of lies the devil has put together to deceive even the elect—God's chosen. (Mk 13:22) It is a very dangerous philosophy because a lack of absolutes makes it easy for humanism to justify iniquity—existential offspring.

Terrorism in the world is driven, not so much by religious belief, as by an existential mind-set that recognizes no law but the law of an old heart filled with self-love and evil. Jesus warns us that in the last days, because "iniquity shall abound, the love of many shall grow cold." (Mt 24:12) God help us!

> And whoever falls on this stone will be broken; but on whomever it falls, it will grind him to powder."
>
> Matthew 21:44

Pr. Tom Schaller:

This Holy Bible gives us God's absolute Word on what will happen to those who refuse to allow the light of the glorious Gospel of Christ to shine unto them. (2Co 4:4) I'm watching this happen in life all around me. People think there's a neutral place. There is not! They either fall on the rock of their salvation (Ps 62:2-6) and they're broken, and get a new heart and a renewed mind, or the rock of God's judgment falls upon them, and—I'm saying it—and I'm saying it very seriously...I'm saying it in all reality: The rock will fall, and it will grind unbelieving people to powder. God is not playing a game! Life is not a game! It absolutely is a very serious matter.

God has mercy upon us at the Cross; there is no mercy whatsoever otherwise! Without the Savior, no mercy from God! Yes, I have my gains, and my religion, and my concepts, and whatever else it is that I have, but—make no mistake about it— judgment is on its way as you read these words; its only a matter of time before it arrives, and that time is short. (1Co 7:29, 1Pe 4:7)

There absolutely is a Heaven, there absolutely is a hell, and there absolutely is a Savior.

> The Lord is not slack concerning his promise, as some men count slackness; but is longsuffering to us-ward, not willing that any should perish, but that all should come to repentance.
>
> 2 Peter 3:9

There is a period of God's long-suffering, but a rock of judgment is absolutely coming down from the Great White Throne. (Re 20:11-15) People will be cast into an absolute hell called a lake of fire, (Re 21:14) where there absolutely will be much, much, much weeping and gnashing of teeth forever. (Mt 8:12, 22:13, 24:51, 25:30, Lu 13:28)

I pray to the Lord that I'll always have a burden for souls entrapped in sin and iniquity in this world; drug addiction, murders, rapes, city slums, white-collar crime, divorces, abused children, tragedy upon tragedy, suffering upon suffering! With this burden I implore you: God is real! Awake, you who sleep! (Ep 5:14) God is absolutely real and so is His love!

If you never have before, or even if you think that somehow you may have, but you're just not so sure; then you desperately need to receive Christ, and His love. He created you with this need; you can never be complete until it is fulfilled. You're complete in Him, and in Him only. (Co 2:10) Christ in you is your only hope of glory. (Co 1:27) Without Him, no matter who you are, or what you are, or how much you have, or what Church you go to, or what your religious beliefs are; no matter how many good works you have done, how much money you've given, how good your intentions are; you are as nothing, spiritually speaking. That does not mean God does not love you—He absolutely does, but until you receive that love, you're absolutely, altogether without God and without hope in this present world. (Ep 2:12)

Are you born again? If you want to go to Heaven when you die you must be born again (Jn 3:3-7) and you can be—not by joining a church, being baptized, being a good person, or any thing you can or cannot do— only by believing Jesus Christ is who He says He is: The Messiah—your Savior. If you never have before, I implore you, receive Him now by saying this simple prayer of faith. Speak the words; let your ears hear them that they may sink into the very depths of your heart and soul:

> Heavenly Father, thank you for Jesus!
> I know I am a sinner.

> ————

> Lord Jesus, I believe you;
> I believe you died for all my sins,
> past, present, and future;
> I receive you as my Savior.
> Come into my life.

Fill my heart with your precious love.
Make me the person you created me to be.
Fill me with your Holy Spirit,
Give me eternal life,
And take me to Heaven to be with
you when I die.

Thank you, Jesus!

Amen!

*And if you said that prayer and really meant it,
you are absolutely a WINNER in Christ Jesus!
Love A L W A Y S Wins!*

Chapter 5
— God's Love—Our Health —

Love And Obedience

My wife, Margie, works all day and I'm retired, so I spend a lot of time home alone. Remembering the old adage, *"A dog is a man's best friend"*, I thought it might be a nice to have a puppy around the house to keep me company. So I just went online one day and began to browse around under "puppies" and there they were, thousands to choose from, every size, shape and color imaginable. But I happened upon a cute, little, 8-week-old, black & white, Boston Terrier, and that was it! If you like puppy's (and who doesn't) he really is a very nice puppy. Out of thousands of possibilities, I picked out that particular one. And it actually was a bit more than I could afford, but I didn't care. I wanted that puppy! So I got out my credit card and ordered it—special delivery, no less. Then I just could not wait until I had that little dog in my hands. When I finally did, I was very happy— and so was the puppy—needless to say. And what do you think I named the puppy? *Puppi!* Of course! And Puppi knows his master as, *Daddy*.

Created in God's own image and likeness, (Ge 1:26) we really are much like Him (though we certainly are not God) and God is much like us. Somewhere in eternity, before ever the world was created, He decided He wanted a human; someone like Him that He could share His love with, someone who would respond to Him, and glorify Him in Love. (Ge 1:26) In his omniscient mind, He began to browse through all of time and space until He happened upon you, and that was it! Out of all the squillions of possibilities His eternal mind could imagine, God created *you*. Now, you were very expensive; but He decided you were worth whatever it cost, and He went to work creating you on that very day. (Ge 1:27, 2:7, 22-22) It would only be a matter of a few thousand years—no problem for God—and you would actually be in His loving hands. He also made billions of people similar to you, but each one entirely unique. (Ep 2:10) Then one day you arrived—you were born—and you began to do all the little things you naturally do (which we won't get into) yet it pleased Him to pay the price. (Is 53:10) And to this day He loves you with an absolute, perfect, unconditional love as He did the first time He saw you in eternity. (Je 31:3) Not to say that you are sinless, and you know sin does have its consequence, but in God's eyes you can do no wrong; there's never a time when you're not under His omnipotent hand. His love for you will never fail, and you are His very own, unique, irreplaceable, masterpiece of creation! (Ep 2:10)

> Even as [in His love] He chose us [actually picked us out for Himself as His own] in Christ before the foundation of the world, that we should be holy (consecrated and set apart for Him) and blameless in His sight, even above reproach, before Him in love.
>
> Ephesians 1:4 (Amplified)

God picked us out for Himself to be His own in Christ. This was our position before time began; before we're conceived in our mother's womb, we are His elect. Yes, we are conceived in sin, (Ps 51:5) born sinners, but we are predestinated to be born-again of the Spirit; (Jo 3:3-5) called, justified, glorified, (Ro 8:28-30) and seated above in Heavenly places in Christ Jesus. (Ep 2:6)

And God in Christ paid for the sin that separated us from Him (2Co 5:19) with His sinless human blood; we are bought with a price, (1Co 6:20, 7:23) we are His people, the sheep—or we might say, puppies—of his hand, (Ps 95:7) He is our God and, in our position, we are indeed set apart for Him and blameless in His sight, even above reproach before Him in Love. Yes, we're sinners every day of our life but that's only our experience—the life of the old heart. The desire of our new heart, which always operates from its position, is to walk with Him in the Spirit, (Ro 8:4; Ga 5:16, 25) in the newness of our life in Christ, (Ro 6:4) to take up our cross daily and follow Him. (Lu 9:2)

Now, my Puppi knows a few tricks; he's actually a very smart, obedient little dog. How did I train him so well? The secret is in always having a supply of Puppi's favorite treats in hand. One day I was showing off Puppi's tricks and I looked at him and said, Puppi! ...Sit! Instantly Puppi obeyed, and was immediately rewarded with a little doggy-treat from Daddy's hand. A few minutes later I gave Puppi the command to sit again, and he obeyed, but when he was offered the treat, it was refused. What? Once again, he was commanded: Sit! And again Puppi obeyed instantly but still refused the treat. This was interesting because if Puppi was only being obedient in order to get a treat, why did he obey when he wasn't interested in a treat at all? It must be for one reason: Puppi loves Daddy, and just wants to please him—treat or no treat! Now that is good; and it's important because as we walk together, sometimes Puppi's obedience is a matter of life or death, and there's no time for a treat.

This is actually what God wants for us. He's training us to respond to His love automatically—without hesitation, and our obedience is connected to His love, just like Puppi's obedience is connected to Daddy's love. And sometimes our obedience really is a matter of life or death, not just getting a treat. Daddy loves Puppi, but God loves people way more.

We're being trained to reign with the Lord Jesus Christ, (2Tim 2:12; Rev 5:10; Rev 20:4-6, 22:5) and there's a phase of training where obedience almost always gets blessed, but training also takes us beyond obedience to Love. Only when obedience has become an automatic response to Love are we fully operational in God's channel of charity. Obedience must become faith-obedience—obedience just because we Love God and always want to please Him. (He 11:6) By faith we respond to every initiation of His love; we love to obey Love because faith-obedience produces the greatest blessing of all: Blessing God Himself!

You are one eternally secure little puppy in His love!

5

The New Heart—Love's Link To Thought

> By having the eyes of your heart flooded with light, so that you can know and understand the hope to which He has called you, and how rich is His glorious inheritance in the saints (His set-apart ones).
>
> Ephesians 1:18 (Amplified)

> *We should no longer be children, tossed to and fro and carried about with every wind of doctrine, by the trickery of men, in the cunning craftiness of deceitful plotting, but, speaking the truth in love, may grow up in all things into Him who is the head—Christ—from whom the whole body, joined and knit together by what every joint supplies, according to the effective working by which every part does its share, causes growth of the body for the edifying of itself in love.*
>
> Ephesians 4:14-16

When the Bible refers to the Church, it can mean any or all of three different entities: the *individual* believer, the *local* assembly, or the *universal* fellowship. In this text it could be likened to a human body by the fact that all its parts are tightly linked together in a specific purpose, which is the building up of itself in His love. This love links every part of our soul with the heart just as it links every individual in the local assembly with every other individual, and every local assembly together with every other assembly, to comprise the universal Church.

Love is the unifying element of the Body of Christ including every member. This is a very important truth because outside of the Body, people are tossed about like ships on a stormy sea, by every wind of doctrine the world, the flesh, and the devil can devise. (Ep 4:14) Love also unifies the government of the soul—mind, volition, emotions, conscience, and self-consciousness—all of which are very vulnerable to fragmentation and iniquity when Love is missing.

> This I say, therefore, and testify in the Lord, that you should no longer walk as the rest of Gentiles walk, in the futility of their mind, having their understanding darkened, being alienated from the life of God, because of the ignorance that is in them, because of the blindness of their heart...
>
> Verses 17-18

The correlation of Ephesians 1:18 and 4:14-18 provide us with the link between the mind (human thought) and *agape* love, which is literally the essence of the new heart of every born-again believer.

When a man has lighted a candle, he doesn't put it under a bushel, but on a candlestick, that the light may be visible to all. (Mt 5:14-16) The light of the body is the eye, and when the eye is single, the whole body is full of light. (Lu 11:33-34) When the spiritual eye is single—fixated upon Him only—our entire being—body, soul, and spirit—is lighted by Love. It fills our personality; our eyes become as lenses that focus and radiate Love. It is an amazing thing, but we have often heard it said when we Love unbelievers:

"There's something about you..."
And we say, "Yes, we know,
its God's Love, Our Health."

5

A Miracle At The Gate Beautiful

> Now Peter and John went up together to the temple at the hour of prayer, the ninth hour. ² And a certain man lame from his mother's womb was carried, whom they laid daily at the gate of the temple which is called Beautiful, to ask alms from those who entered the temple; ³ who, seeing Peter and John about to go into the temple, asked for alms.
>
> Acts 3:1-3

Peter and John were on their way to the Temple to pray, and a certain man who was lame from birth was begging at the gate called *Beautiful*. The beggar probably already knew them to be charitable men and he didn't hesitate to ask for alms—Greek, *eleemosynea*: a gift for the poor and needy—charity. And could it be that "charity" is a Holy Spirit play-on-words pointing to Love? Because Love is this man's real need and it is about to be the instrument of his healing; we're talking about God's Love, Our Health.

> And Peter, fastening his eyes upon him with John said Look on us. And he gave heed unto them, expecting to receive something of them.
>
> Verses 4-5

The Spirit moved Peter and John to fix their eyes upon the beggar because that would stir up their compassion for the man. We might imagine that they would have a flash back of themselves before Jesus came into their own life. As they gazed upon this poor, crippled beggar they saw much more than the poverty and the physical handicap; they saw themselves ...without Love. And are we not all born into the world as beggars, crippled and spiritually poverty stricken by original sin—let alone personal sin?

"Look on us", demanded Peter; he wants the beggar's eyes to meet his own. Is this a primary means of transmitting Love? Yes, for we all have experienced this grace many times when God would minister to us on a very personal level, especially in a time of need. Now the beggar gave heed to them, only because he was expecting alms, but divine love working through Peter is like a laser beam of mystical, beautiful light, and it penetrates the depths of the darkness of this poor, crippled soul.

> Then Peter said, Silver and gold have I none; but such as I have give I thee: In the name of Jesus Christ of Nazareth rise up and walk.
>
> Verse 6

What did Peter have to give the beggar? It wasn't silver, and it wasn't gold; it wasn't anything he hadn't already received from Heaven. It could only be the glory of Love shining out from a Spirit-filled heart. When the beggar looked into the eyes of Peter, and then again into John's eyes, he saw the love of the Lord Jesus Christ—twice, a double dose—as though to make sure he knew it was the real thing. It was like a beacon from a lighthouse on a stormy night at sea—which for this beggar began the day he was born—and it suddenly touched his wounded heart...When we meet this beggar in Heaven his heart will still be singing it:

I thank God for the lighthouse.
I owe my life to him.
Jesus is the lighthouse,
And from the rocks of sin,
He has shown his light around me
That I might clearly see.
If it wasn't for the lighthouse, tell me,
Where would this ship be?

The wonder of *agape* love's power to heal is an indescribable blessing that one must experience in order to fully appreciate. God has systematically prepared our soul for a moment in time when we will experience Love for the very first time. (2Co 6:2; He 4:7) Then we're like this beggar, crippled from birth, waiting at a gate called Beautiful—or we might say, Mount Zion, the throne of the great King—where Love in person is indeed beautiful for the situation. (Ps 48:1-2) And maybe you're only looking for an answer to a prayer—we might say alms, "a Puppi-treat"—or even "charity"—but God's plan is to give us much more than we could ever ask or think, that we might be filled with all the fullness of God— love unfeigned. (2Co 6:6; 1Pe 1:22)

> To know the love of Christ which passes knowledge; that you may be filled with all the fullness of God. Now to Him who is able to do exceedingly abundantly above all that we ask or think, according to the power that works in us.
>
> Ephesians 3:19

For many years this beggar's daily routine was to go to the gate called Beautiful and beg; he had it down to a science and was very successful at it in this locale. I can imagine that he prayed often that passers-by would be moved with compassion and generosity toward him, and they often were. Truth be known, at times he was thinking that those who were giving alms were actually beggars also, on their way to the temple to ask for blessings for themselves—not that he wasn't thankful for them, but he was right in more ways than one, and spiritually speaking he might as well have been Puppi doing tricks for treats. He had no clue that on a certain day God had a plan to take him, and many with him, (Ac 4:4) beyond a treat, to the truth.

At first he only obeyed Peter's command to look at them; experience had taught him well; be sensitive about eye contact with prospective benefactors. But he was suddenly aware of something very unusual about the way these men looked at him. And it struck his heart like a bolt of lightning! He saw a new level of love in the eyes of both Peter and John, and he understood instantaneously, in his heart, that it was the real thing; he knew he was truly loved.

It is so very clear to us: His love-starved soul instinctively recognized, received, and responded to Love. Instantly—before ever he knew what happened—he had a new heart and a new spirit. (Ez 36:26) And there was light...Love commanded it: *Let there be light; and there was light!* (Gen 1:3) The light of Love penetrated the darkness of his mind; he was enraptured with the sheer beauty of it, so much so, that at first he didn't even realize that Love had healed him physically... but Peter knew:

> And he took him by the right hand, and lifted [him] up: and immediately his feet and anklebones received strength. And he leaping up stood, and walked, and entered with them into the temple, walking, and leaping, and praising God.
>
> Acts 3:7-8

The beggar was only looking for a treat, but God's plan is always to treat us to a blessing abundantly above and beyond anything can we ask or think. (Ep 3:20) Leaping and walking and praising God, He rejoiced and entered into the temple with the others—into the fellowship of the Body of Christ—on his own two feet!

The power of Love working in us
is the greatest power in the universe,
and it is desperate with desire to bless us
and others in the process.

5

Love Thinks

> Though I speak with the tongues of men and of angels,
> but have not love, I have become sounding brass or a
> clanging cymbal.

1 Corinthians 13:1

If I'm talking and do not have Love, what is the source of my words? It must be the old heart, [Mt 12:34,Lu 6:45] and it will often be emotions expressing feelings in some way because human love has its source in our emotions only. Contrariwise, *agape* is not a *feeling* love, it is a *thinking* love, and the emotions are connected to thought, but are never in authority over the new heart. How does *agape* think? It thinks via doctrine—the mind of Christ.

> And though I have the gift of prophecy, and understand
> all mysteries and all knowledge, and though I have all
> faith, so that I could remove mountains, but have not
> love, I am nothing.

Verse 2

Pr. Tom Schaller:

Maybe I have most amazing gifts: prophecy and knowledge, mountain moving faith, religion, every category of doctrine our ministry teaches—all memorized, 30 years of experience on a mission field, many good friends in the local assembly, respect and honor; but it's possible withal that I'm totally unable to think with God.

Let's say for instance that I lust after a certain woman; what did Jesus say about this? Not good! (Mt 5:28) Where does lust originate? Out of the darkened depths of the old heart (Mk 7:20-23—the home of the sin nature; the fallen nature that is residual in the flesh until physical death. So what do I do when this lust flashes through my mind? I stop it dead in its tracks, I close the door on that thought, and I take it captive and bring it to the obedience of Christ, where thoughts originate with *agape*. (2Co 10:4-6) I'm able to do this because the old sin nature is no longer in charge. (Rom 6:10-14) Thoughts that come from my old heart no longer define who I am—Love does that. I am not my sin! God is love—Love occupies the throne of my life in my new heart, and love does not think lustful thoughts.

What is the basis of my life in the new heart? It is absolutely Love. I've been given a new heart by grace wherein I stand, (1Pe 5:12) I have a totally new life, (2Co 5:17; Ep 4:24; Co 3:10) and I died yet I live—not by my strength—but by the faith of Christ who gave himself for me, who lives in me, and loves me, (Ga 2:20) and has poured His love into my heart. (Ro 5:5) So how many times can I sin in one day? How much of my old man can I live with in one day knowing that he is crucified with Christ, that the body of sin might be destroyed, that henceforth I might not serve sin. (Ro 6:6-8) Many there be who can live in the old man for years, even a lifetime, and never deal with him—never put on the new man created in righteousness and true holiness, (Ep 4:24) renewed in knowledge after the image of Him who created him, (Co 3:10) and therefore, never come to know the grace of God that teaches us to deny ungodliness and the lust of the flesh. (Ti 2:11-12 Sad, but very true because His love truly is our health in more ways than we know.

And I can have the gift of prophecy, I can understand all mystery, have all knowledge and all faith. I could be

147

very proud—as leaders can be—if I live in my old man; my speaking and words being very eloquent, and in all things be correct, yet I actually do not live in God's love; therefore, I'm incorrect, I'm nothing, and all that I ever do actually counts for nothing in Heaven.

> And though I bestow all my goods to feed the poor, and though I give my body to be burned, but have not love, it profits me nothing.
>
> Verse 3

Self-sacrifice is pathetic because it profits me absolutely nothing if it's done apart from *agape* love working in and through me every step of the way. Many forms of self-sacrifice—giving the body to be burned—are actually a form of self-interest—something one does for something they get in return. Suicide is an expression of very serious emotional injury rooted in self-interest— i.e. I will have the attention I need, even if have to kill myself to get it. Pathetic!

The flesh brings much pressure to bear upon the heart in the name of a guilt consciousness, political ploy, community service, religious recognition, and good deeds of all sorts. And we thank God for the good deeds people do, but we (believers) understand that we could spend a lifetime doing good works in the strength of the sin nature, and the sum total of its value would be absolute zero in terms of God's reality at the judgment seat of Christ. (2Co 5:10) I could be saved, a born-again believer, have my name written in the Lamb's Book of Life, be Spirit filled, and have a new heart filled with God's love, but if the operation of Love is missing from my Christian service— however awesome that may be—it will be accounted as worthless wood, hay, or stubble and will quickly perish in the fires of judgment. (2CO 3:9-15) I believe this means that, by the mercy of God, my memory of it will be deleted— erased from all remembrance forever. (Re 7:17, 21:4)

For the born-again believer, there will be amazing rewards in Heaven for every good work, but only if it is done by faith through grace, (Ep 2:8-9) and in the strength of Love. (Mt 10:42; Lu 12:33-34; 2Co 5:10-14; He 13:20-21; Re 14:13)

Pr. Tom Schaller:

The good thing about sharing these truths is that they're not far from us. We see them in the midst of our Church and we know they're directly from God, as we do live in this message every day. We have a lot of activity going on in our church but we're not driven by activity; every work is a work of faith and a labor of Love. (1Th 1:3) We continually, quietly relate everything we do to receiving God's love and pouring it out to one another. This kind of work produces a very healthy church."

Therefore as we fluctuate between the old man and the new, (Ro 7) we're ever quick to deal with our sins, bring our life boldly before God without introspection or presumption, confess our failure, walk in the light, fellowship under the Blood, and be edified in *agape* love. (Lu 11:13)

4 Love suffers long and is kind...

Verse 4

Have you ever met someone, who has a problem and wants it fixed right now? Sometimes it's a question they want answered, and they want the answer 'NOW!' Or a husband says I need her to be a better wife...starting yesterday! But if our emotions connect with doctrine they will be led into an attitude of peace, quietness, security, edification, and positive feeling.

Or I could make decisions based upon truth that is not connected to feelings, like ten of the twelve spies who went to check out the Promised Land. (Nu 13:17-33) They all saw the same land but ten came back with a bad report—giants, walled cities, etc.—but two of them, Joshua and Caleb, came back saying, "We can take the land; lets do it right now." (Nu 13:30)

Sad things do happen—death, addiction, lost jobs, marriage failures, lies, etc. But if God is in us, we have Love in us, and the option to look at life in the light of Love, because this love thinks. Twelve saw the same problem but two saw it in a different light and their report is very different. It wasn't that the two didn't see the problems, but also saw beyond the problems to someone greater than the problems—God who Loves them...and promised them that land.

A man could be married to a woman but his love for her is only human love—not *agape* based—if he's not a believer, he cannot not see her thru the eyes of *agape*; instead he sees her with a spirit of fault finding. He dwells upon her faults, talks about them, and constantly reminds her of them. Or maybe a man has a job where he sees real problems every day, and complains to management about them; expresses his frustration, takes the problems home with him, complains about them there, and everywhere he goes. Or maybe someone at home complains about bad neighbors to the rest of the family—and maybe its true—but innocent children are aghast at all the negativity, and do not understand. These are examples of day-to-day details of life where people perceive problems in the light of their emotions without ever considering them from a divine viewpoint of love. But *agape* has a way of putting a different construct on problematic situations and circumstances.

Love has a profound effect upon every soul it touches. It is literally the most powerful force in the entire universe. What the world needs to deal with multiple, diverse, complicated, numerous, enormous problems... is Love—*agape love, our health.*

Pr. Tom Schaller:

One fallen man can be a terror to many. One bad report from ten negative people discouraged everyone in Israel—literally millions! (Nu 14:1-4) Joshua and Caleb lived in the presence of all the negativity of Israel for forty long years. But Love suffers long, and is kind in the process. How long will you or I tolerate a negative person? How long will we live with a problem person? How much can we take? And how long will God tolerate the human race??

Often enough in our Church there are many problems and difficulties to deal with every day. But *agape* love in our hearts never fails. There are giants in the land—yes, there are—but we can do it; let's go for it...now! Lets be like Joshua and Caleb; let's receive His love and let that love do our thinking and make our decisions. And we will be amazed at the results.

We will pray on the way:

Lord, you are awesome; your love suffers long, it is kind, not envious, not puffed up, does not behave badly, is not arrogant, is not driven by anything, is not self-seeking, is not easily provoked, and thinks no evil. Your love is our health!

What if Jesus Christ came without this love? How long would he stay with us? By the time he was ten he would be saying: "Do I need this? Nope! I'm otta here...See y'all!" But, no! He stayed with it; thirty years of preparation and three years of a dynamite ministry of Love that ended on the Cross, where Love was perfected and became the standard of all ministry—God's love, our health!

When one goes to Bible College they have a need to be patient in preparation. There is always a ministry ahead of us, but we must first learn to love with the love of the Lord in every situation. Two of twelve—one of six—will need to wait 40 years before they get a chance to enter into the Promised Land, then they go! Then they say, "I told you so. I knew we could do it forty years ago. I knew it but you would not believe—would not listen to that message—because you did not know the nature of God—love unfeigned." (2Co 6:1-6) But you live in your wounds, your injuries, your concentration on faults and problems, you complain constantly and emote with human love, having no clue as to how to think beyond your cares and woes with God who is sovereign above all of them. In our Bible College we learn to live in meditation, (Ps 1:1-2) responding to Love, worshipping God, learning of Him, praying, learning how to receive His love, and minister His love in the midst of the Body of Christ.

God put a thorn in Paul's flesh in order to teach him how to be humble and receive grace. (2Co 12:7-9) And he prayed diligently for that thorn to be removed, but God's only response was: "My grace is sufficient for you...My love is thinking, Paul; think with me, know that you are Loved, receive that grace, and Love others whose love only knows how to emote. You will need to suffer long, Paul—for as long as it takes—and you will need to be kind while you do so. And you will forget the thorn as you minister Love. My grace will be sufficient; Love will be your health."

> [Love] does not rejoice in iniquity, but rejoices in truth...
>
> Verse 6

The world rejoices in iniquity because it deceives itself with mythological love, which is based upon mythological faith. It's faith that is in itself only, and really isn't faith at all, only an exercise in *lust*. (1Jn 2:16) But Love rejoices in truth, never in evil speaking, or uncovering, or slandering, or digging-up dirt about others; (Ps 64) it is rejoicing in something higher, it is rejoicing in truth and the nature of God who is Love. Bearing all things, believing all things, hoping all things, and casting the most positive light on all things.

> *Love is the sufficiency of grace*
> *that sees beyond the thorn*
> *to the Throne*
> *and the Truth*

Pr. Tom Schaller:

Let's be careful about the words we use in one another's presence—even at home. Husbands, wives, children; be careful what you say to each other. Love one another with the love of the Lord. Be Love-thinkers in the work place; regardless of how others speak to you, speak words of Love to them, relate to them through eyes of Love. In your mind you're quiet as you're processing words that edify with Love; and as you have occasion to speak you do so in wisdom and in truth. (Ep 4:15)

5

At The Table of Love

When the dust of the wars in Judah had settled, King David asked: "Is there any left of the house of Saul that is still alive?" (2 Sa 9:1) And he was informed of Mephibosheth—Saul's grandson by Jonathan—who was lame in both feet. David sent his servants to bring Mephibosheth to him, and when he arrived he was immediately accepted as one of the family and did eat at David's table for the rest of his natural life. (2Sa 9:10)

Mephibosheth is like us; his lameness in both feet represents that ugly crippled part of our life that is unable to walk the talk, and is often offensive in the midst of the Body, the family of God. But under the King's table—the table of God's love—this is not visible. At the table of grace, regardless of our handicap, we only see one another with Love. We know there are some broken legs under the table but we don't see them.

David saw beyond the victories he had won, to the covenant he made with Jonathan many years earlier. (1Sa 18:1-3) He had an attitude of Love that covers a multitude of sins. (Pr 10:12; 1Pe 4:8) This is the way Jesus sees us—in spite of our handicap of sin—in the light of Love that never fails because it thinks no evil, and rejoices—not in iniquity—but in truth. And this is the way we see one another in the Body, not on the basis of a fault we happen to know about, but on the basis of New Covenant Love. We see each other through a new heart that looks beyond our fault to our need for Love, a heart that knows the nature of God who is Love, and therefore sees others as He does. We Love one another as He loves us; we Love Mephibosheth, and we prepare a place for him. We may be disappointed in him at times—as we often are with one who just can't keep the pace—but Love is patient, suffers long, and is kind.

Where would we be if it were not for the long suffering of the Lord? Where would David be? Where would Mephibosheth be? Where would I be? Where would freedom be, where would our vision be, where would faith be, where would hope be? Where would anyone be? ...But Love bears all things, and hopes all things; this is Love that is the essence of our total health.

If a limp slows somebody down, we have a purpose in our new heart to not look under the table of Love with evil thinking. Our new heart thinks with God in categories of doctrine, in terms of Love that rejoices in truth. When we have the mind of Christ in us it never fails to manifest something the world is very hungry for—a love that does not have its source in human feelings, a love that has the mind that made the sun, the moon, the stars, and you and I, a love that cannot fail us even though we may fail ourselves and even God who is Love.

Pr. Tom Schaller:

I love my wife; she is beautiful, and she is very important to me. I remember it well, the day I married her, the hope in my heart for a family, happy and blessed of God's love. I can never be disappointed in her or our children because I love them with a love that cannot, and will not, ever fail. This love must be learned. It is in us but we must submit to it—receive it freely—because we fluctuate to another heart that is not of God and does not know this love at all.

We prophesy, we move mountains with our faith, we speak with the tongue of learned men and even angels, but we have not Love. And when we're hurt we hurt back. When you disappoint me I look under the table right away and tell you what I think of you. When I'm injured I live in the thought of that injury and never shake it off—never let it go—and I'm never free from it. I have not Love and I do not live as a believer—I live in a different world, another life that God did not give, and certainly does not expect me to suffer through. This is not love that suffers long and is kind.

Someone who has not Love will say: "Hey, get a life!" But they do not know that we have...the life! We bear one another's burdens, (Ga 6:2) we lay down our lives for one another, (1Jn 3:16) we Love one another as He Loves us, (Jn 15:9-12) and we never think evil—never one time do we look under the table! This is the life! And what a life it is! We feel it, we know it, and we just sit around the table of Love and pack it away—fellowship filets, grace cakes, mercy pudding, and piece pie for dessert—we just thrive on the fruit of Love. Don't look under the table; you might not like what you see, but on top of the table.... O, my! Yum—yum—Yummmmm!

Mephibosheth would say: "I eat here every day; the food is awesome. I do need someone to pick me up and put me at the table, but once I'm here...Wow! And I don't even have a job! How awesome is that kind of love? God is good; He brought me to His banqueting table, and His banner over me is...LOVE! (SS 2:4) ...Pass the grace cakes over this way, please! Thank you, Uncle Dave."

The world, the flesh, and the devil may beat you to a pulp but this love will never fail you. It will keep you, and bless you, and use you, and make you healthy, and never fail you. (1Co 13:8) It's the life of Christ in us—our hope and our glory (Co 1:27)—the very health of body, and soul, and spirit.

We're very strong!
Very well able to go up and take hold of every-
thing God gave us,
because we have it:
LOVE — our very Health!

Chapter 6
– Love Liberates Us –
– From Problems of Knowledge –

The More Excellent Way

A woman of Samaria came to draw water. Jesus said to her, "Give Me a drink." For His disciples had gone away into the city to buy food. Then the woman of Samaria said to Him, "How is it that you, being a Jew, ask a drink from me, a Samaritan woman?" For Jews have no dealings with Samaritans. Jesus answered and said to her, "If you knew the gift of God, and whom it is who says to you, 'Give Me a drink,' you would have asked Him, and He would have given you living water." The woman said to Him, "Sir, You have nothing to draw with, and the well is deep. Where then do you get that living water? Are you greater than our father Jacob, who gave us the well, and drank from it himself, as well as his sons and his livestock?" Jesus answered and said to her, "Whoever drinks of this water will thirst again, but whomever drinks of the water that I shall give him will never thirst. But the water that I shall give him will become in him a fountain of water springing up into everlasting life." The woman said to Him, "Sir, give me this water, that I may not thirst, nor come here to draw." Jesus said to her, "Go, call your husband, and come here." The woman answered and said, "I have no husband." Jesus said to her, "You have well said, 'I have no husband,' for you have had five husbands, and the one whom you now have is not your husband; in that you spoke truly." The woman said to Him, "Sir, I perceive that you are a prophet. Our fathers worshiped on this mountain, and you Jews say that in Jerusalem is the place where one ought to worship." Jesus said to her, "Woman, believe me, the hour is coming when you will neither on this mountain, nor in Jerusalem, worship the Father. You worship what you do not know; we know what we worship, for salvation is of the Jews. God [is] Spirit, and those who worship Him must worship in spirit and truth." But the hour is coming, and now is, when the true worshipers will worship the Father in spirit and truth, for the Father is seeking such to worship Him. The woman said to Him, "I know that Messiah is coming" (who is called Christ). "When He comes, He will tell us all things." Jesus said to her, "I who speak to you am He."

John 4:7-26

Pr. Tom Schaller:

The words of the Samaritan woman reveal a strong *natural* orientation. Natural thinking always reveals a natural heart; (Mt 12:34; Lu 6:45) but Jesus is leading her—challenging her natural concepts of spiritual information.

By God's grace we do live in a nice neighborhood but there's a college men's dorm at the end of the street that can be a bit boisterous at times. Some have even called the police to come and quiet them down on occasion. My wife brought it to my attention that their graduation would soon be coming up and many of them would be leaving; that I should share the Gospel with them while they're still here in the neighborhood. I thought about that, and one day, as I was about to pull out onto the main street, there they were—out in the back yard of their dorm. So I went around the block, parked the car near them, and just sat there for a few minutes to prayerfully consider how I might approach seven, young college graduates who have been drinking and partying here in our neighborhood all year long...Then I got out and spoke to them: "Hi, men! How are ya today?" And I began sharing the Gospel with them as led of the

Lord. It was amazing how words of faith came from my heart to minister Love and grace right there on the spot. I don't know whether or not what I shared will ultimately get them saved but I am sure that their natural concepts of God were challenged by supernatural love. I couldn't help but think that this was much like Jesus talking to a Samaritan woman at the well:

"You can't be asking me for water, Sir! Because you're a Jew and I'm a Samaritan... You know we don't talk to one another, don't you?"

"I have no husband..."

"We worship on this mountain; you say we should worship in Jerusalem..."

Knowledge! These statements reveal knowledge, but its knowledge from a natural heart, which can be, and often is, a major barrier to a ministry of Love.

1 Corinthians, Chapters 1-11, deals with Church carnality. The Corinthians had knowledge, and they were spiritual, but they had many deep, serious problems. In 1 Corinthians 12:1 there is a shift in theme to a very important word that defines spirituality:

> Now concerning spiritual gifts, brethren, I do not want you to be ignorant...
>
> 1 Corinthians 12:1

"Spiritual [gifts]" is translated from the Greek, *pneumatikos,* meaning: spirituality relating to the human spirit as that part of a person that is an instrument of God; i.e. the new heart of a believer.

Paul is saying to Corinthian believers: I do not want you to be ignorant (Greek, *agnoeo*: without knowledge) and I'm glad you're not, but I would that your knowledge always be in the proper context—*pneumatikos.*

Two other words used in the New Testament to delineate knowledge are *soul* (Greek, *pseukikos*: the soulish (inner, natural) man, 6 times) and *flesh* (Greek, *sarkikos*: the carnal (outward, fleshly man, 11times). So there are essentially three perspectives on knowledge: 1) the flesh (world-conscious), 2) the soul (self-conscious), or 3) the spirit (God-conscious).

In the original language Paul's tone at the end of Chapter 12 is *mocking* knowledgeable Corinthian believers for their emphasis on spiritual gifts while many are yet carnal; they love to talk about their spirituality but the way they perceive knowledge reveals much carnality and worldliness.

> Now you are the body of Christ, and members individually. And God has appointed these in the church: first apostles, second prophets, third teachers, after that miracles, then gifts of healings, helps, administrations, varieties of tongues. Are all apostles? Are all prophets? Are all teachers? Are all workers of miracles? Do all have gifts of healings? Do all speak with tongues? Do all interpret? But earnestly desire the best gifts. And yet I show you a more excellent way.
>
> 1 Corinthians 12:27-31

Paul is saying: "Oh, you say we ought to all be spiritual, don't you? You're the knowledgeable ones always talking about spirituality (*pneumatikos*), aren't you?" [And the Bible uses *pneumatikos* 25 times—11 times in the letter to the Corinthians. Paul has purposely led us through this chapter up to ...a more excellent way (Greek, *hyperbole*: a way that is beyond natural perspective)]. "Well I'm glad you are knowledgeable—everybody has knowledge—but let me introduce you to the key to managing your knowledge; it's called, Love!"

Now we have the Bible's word on "Love"; but actually God's Word on Love is the Bible. God is Love, [1Jn 4:8,16] and the Holy Spirit is Love and He is our constant

Comforter [Jn 14:16-18]—for we have an accuser, accusing us to God, and accusing God to us—the devil who stands before God day and night to accuse of sin and iniquity. [Re 12:11]

And who really cares about us? The Psalmist looks to his right, then to his left, but he can find no man who knows him, or cares for his soul. [Ps 142:4] But Jesus knows us, [Jn 10:14-15, 27] and he does care about us. [1Pe 5:7] He is our advocate—who is also before God (The Judge, no less!) interceding for us; [1Jn 2:1] and no charge whatsoever can be brought against us. How so? Because our status with The Judge is on the basis of the shed Blood of His only begotten Son.

We've been brought into the Family of God where Love—the more excellent way—has made us secure. This is an amazing, incomprehensible, unfathomable Love! We need to hear about it continually in order to just begin to grasp the power of its work in and through our lives.

1 Corinthians 14 concerns the edification of the Body of Christ by the moving and ministry of the Holy Spirit.

1 Corinthians 15 is a brilliant work regarding our identity in the 2nd Adam—Jesus Christ—and our eternal security in his love.

Thus we have a thorough teaching concerning knowledge, and we see that not all knowledge is bad, but much of it is problematic; knowledge must be managed by Love—the Holy Spirit working in us.

These Chapters instruct us in great truths,
the greatest of which is
...Love
—the more excellent way —
that passes ALL knowledge.

6

Love Passes Knowledge

That Christ may dwell in your hearts through faith; that you, being rooted and grounded in love, may be able to comprehend with all the saints what is the width and length and depth and height— to know the love of Christ which passes knowledge; that you may be filled with all the fullness of God.

Ephesians 3:17-19

What do we need to be rooted and grounded in? It's not knowledge—it's Love! Yes, Love is revealed to us through knowledge, but it's knowledge (Greek, *epignosis*: experiential knowledge of Him) that enlightens us in a walk of faith. This knowledge enables us to comprehend the length, width, depth, and height—the time-space, practical application—of the love of Christ that passes knowledge. There is a knowledge that must be passed by Love because, God is Love; we can know His love only in the measure that we can know God, Himself. This is a love that must be experienced—*epignosis*—not taught with words of mere knowledge—*gnosis*—which is knowledge we must be careful with because it can isolate from liberating truth. By faith, this love takes us beyond our worldly experience into a life that transcends time and space—into the fullness of God.

If you wanted to learn how to ski, I could teach you well, because I have a lot of experience on skis and much knowledge that came with that experience —some of it in the *School Of Hard Knocks and Head-Plants*, I must admit. We could talk forever about equipment, clothing, weather, and many of the "do's and do not's" of skiing, but you would never, ever learn to ski until we were out on the mountain together, actually applying all that knowledge. And you might look like a human snowball for a time, but a measure of knowledge would begin to sink in and eventually you would actually enjoy, and have fun skiing. This is what scripture is teaching us: His love passes knowledge—must be experienced in a walk of faith—to even begin to be appreciated for what it is.

I gathered much knowledge during several years in Bible College, and I could quote verses and correlate doctrines with the best of them; even do all the homework, write great papers, and take exams and get an A+ every time. And I actually did that because I was sure the academia would equip me to for ministry...but it did not. Now, all that Bible knowledge was a great asset to me, but it was not enough. It was the application of that knowledge—*epignosis*—on outreaches and mission fields that gave me a grip on Love that serves me—and others through me—to this day. Application of truth produced a passion for the ministry of Love that no amount of knowledge ever could.

We live in the *information age* of this present world, where knowledge is increased on an exponential scale. At present its sum total approximately doubles every 2 years, whereas only a few centuries ago it would take 400 years. The prophet, Daniel, foresaw the later days—which many agree may well be this age—when knowledge would be poured out upon the human race, and people would we traveling to and fro with ease over the entire planet. (Da 12:4) But autonomous knowledge can be very dangerous; we see that in our experience every day. And the world is just beginning to feel the effects of the "knowledge" explosion that will ultimately have an amazingly, profound effect upon it.

> Now concerning things offered to idols: We know that
> we all have knowledge. Knowledge puffs up, but love
> edifies.
>
> 1 Corinthians 8:1

Many have much knowledge of Hinduism, or Taoism, or Communism, or evolution, or creationism, or idolatry; and they like to use it to let everyone know how intellectual they are. Of course knowledge gained in our life experience is useful, but some knowledge is problematical—tricky and sticky.

Mere knowledge puffs us up
like a balloon full of hot air,
but pneumatikos, epignosis fills us up
with all the fullness of God—
LOVE.

Paul would say: I know you have knowledge of idols, [There was much idolatry in the Corinthian world.] ...so what? That kind of knowledge only puffs up the intellect. But who cares for my soul? I know you know about this and that, but tell me: Do you Love me? Because Love edifies, that interests me very much.

We all know how to approach life with a knowledgeable perspective—i.e. religion/idolatry, science, politics, etc., etc. But, tell me about it, do you Love the idolater? Do you Love the person on the outside—the one you can see? Do you Love the guilty? Do you forgive those who injure you?

"I have knowledge about him..."
"O, I know about her..."
"I know their background..."
"I can tell you a few things about that..."

This is *pseukikos* knowledge, natural man talking, but the *pneumatikos*, spiritual man knows something more; he has the Spirit of Love—a working knowledge of the more excellent way.

Samaritan woman: How can you give me a drink of water; you have nothing to draw with, Sir!
Jesus: Oh? Really? Are you sure of that? I can't draw water? Are you sure?
Samaritan woman: Yes, I'm sure! The well is deep; where's your bucket?
Jesus: I do have a bucket. You can't see it, and I know you don't believe it but I do have a bucket.
Samaritan woman: Anyway, you're a Jew and I'm a Samaritan—we're not supposed to be talking, ya know.
Jesus: Is that so? Love can't talk to you? Love can't touch your heart??

There does exists a world which is...
HUGE !
And knowledge cannot touch it,
but LOVE can.

6

Foolish Things Vs Love

Paul: Every one of you Corinthians is divided—alienated from one another. Who is of Paul? Who is of Appolos? Who is of Cephas? Who is of Christ? ...Is Christ divided? Was Paul crucified for you? Were you baptized in Paul's name? (1Co 1:12,13)

Know-it-all: O yeah, he's my man! He's the preacher! I don't know who YOUR Pastor is, but MY Pastor is Paul! ...Apollos, or whomever! And nobody is as knowledgeable as I am; we all know that, don't we?

> Now these things, brethren, I have figuratively transferred to myself and Apollos for your sakes, that you may learn in us not to think beyond what is written, that none of you may be puffed up on behalf of one against the other.
>
> 1 Corinthians 4:6

Paul: I apply all these things about (parties and factions) to Appolos and myself (as an illustration) for your sakes so that you might think of one another in the context of the Word—not going beyond what is written—that none of you will be puffed up with pride, and boasting in favor of one minister over another.

Who's puffed up with pride? Who is Paul referring to?

> I do not write these things to shame you, but as my beloved children I warn you. For though you might have ten thousand instructors in Christ, yet you do not have many fathers; for in Christ Jesus I have begotten you through the gospel.
>
> Verses 14-15

166

Paul: I'm not writing these things to shame you, but to counsel you as my precious children; I know you have 10,000 teachers in Christ, but not many fathers who have begotten you in Christ via the Gospel.

> Now some are puffed up, as though I were not coming to you.
>
> Verse 18

Paul: Some of you are already puffed up with pretension, and pride, and arrogance, spreading the knowledge around that I'm not going to come to you.

Some Corinthians: Who? Paul? Nah! I know Paul! I know about him. He won't be coming here anytime soon. You know that; he's preoccupied with those Jews down there—ministering to religious freaks— then he's over in Asia all the time. He doesn't care about us... I know... I know... I know... Forget Paul! Let's talk about those Diana worshippers. Did you know...

> But I will come to you shortly, if the Lord wills, and I will know, not the word of those who are puffed up, but the power. For the kingdom of God [is] not in word but in power. What do you want? Shall I come to you with a rod, or in love and a spirit of gentleness?
>
> Verses 19-21

Paul: Oh? Really? I know some are puffed up—saying I *will not* come to you; but I *will* come to you—and soon! And when I come I'm not going to be listening to puffed-up, arrogant spirits, I will hear the power of excellence of soul only. Now, which do you prefer? Shall I come to you with a rod of correction, or with Love—the more excellent way? (1Cor 4:19,21)

> *If we come with knowledge*
> *we are likely to be met by knowledge.*
> *If we come with Love*
> *we will surely be met by*
> *Him who is Love.*

Natural preferences cause us to always be looking over our shoulder. Like the ancient Israelites of the Exodus, our preferences will take us right back to the melons, the leeks, the onions, and the garlic of Egypt—the world—if we're not careful with knowledge. (Nu 11:1-6)

Israelites: But we're way out here in the wilderness and all we can think about is melons, and leeks, and onions, and garlic; we want to go back to the bondage of Egypt. Yesterday! Don't you get it, Moses??

Moses: [You have got to be kidding me!] ...What ARE you talking about? What kind of knowledge is that? Don't answer! *Pseukikos!* Don't you know there's a love that passes knowledge—a love that takes us beyond natural things and petty preference?

Pr. Tom Schaller:

I have a friend in Hungary who likes onions and actually eats them like an apple. I tried it once—and I think I would have been OK—but it was just before I went to bed. And I fell asleep but soon woke up; that onion kept coming back up again and again; the smell of it on my breath would wake me right up with tears in my eyes—like I was crying in my sleep. So I gave up on eating raw onions like an apple, but my friend still has that very strange, natural preference.

There was an old oak tree in my back yard; I loved that tree—I have a preference for it...Also for my hometown, my family, my chainsaw, my pickup truck, certain foods, buildings I used to go too—the old school house, the church, people I choose to be my friends...etc.

The Corinthian believers were like this (aren't we all), they had many natural preferences—much knowledge of things they wanted and preferred—but Paul said, "When I come I'm not going to be caring what your preferences are, I only want to know who has the power—power that brings excellence to the soul."

Excellence? Yes, the more excellent way that is Love—a soul that is saturated with the love of the Lord—the power to Love people and not be picky in natural preferences; the power of Love, the power of a vision for the lost, the power to see my God—not my preference—because I need to be edified, not puffed up.

> Where [is] the wise? Where [is] the scribe? Where [is] the disputer of this age? Has not God made foolish the wisdom of this world? For since, in the wisdom of God, the world through wisdom did not know God, it pleased God through the foolishness of the message preached to save those who believe...
>
> 1 Corinthians 1:20-21

And we could add:
"...Lead them on in the faith—to exalt Christ in the Holy Spirit because—"

> Jews request a sign, and Greeks seek after wisdom...
>
> Verse 22

The Israelites waited for a Moses to deliver them from the power of the Egyptian Empire; the Jews waited for another Moses to deliver them from the power of the Roman Empire; the Greeks thought knowledge could deliver them from the power of pride, but all the waiting and thinking and talking about it only puffed them up. And they talked, and talked, and talked, and did nothing but write huge, philosophical, religious books that nobody could understand.

But Jesus didn't come with the power of the sword, he came in the power of the Spirit; he didn't come with wisdom from below, he came with wisdom from above, (Ja 3:15-17) he didn't come with a sign, he came with Love, which is the real thing. And if he speaks to us by the Spirit and by truth, and we hear him, we will be led by real power—the power of Love—the more excellent way—the power of Love, which passes knowledge. Christ came to simple folk—common people who received him gladly (Mk 12:37) by faith, not by knowledge. Without faith it is impossible to please Him. (He 11:6) And whatsoever is not of faith is sin. (Ro 14:23)

Who has the power? We do—born-again, blood-bought, Spirit-filled—We have the power of faith and Love, and it never fails to give us the victory." (1Co 15:67; 1Jn 5:4; Re 15:2)

> We preach Christ crucified, to the Jews a stumbling block and to the Greeks foolishness, but to those who are called, both Jews and Greeks, Christ the power of God and the wisdom of God. Because the foolishness of God is wiser than men, and the weakness of God is stronger than men. For you see your calling, brethren, that not many wise according to the flesh, not many mighty, not many noble, [are called]. But God has chosen the foolish things of the world to put to shame the wise, and God has chosen the weak things of the world to put to shame the things which are mighty; and the base things of the world and the things which are despised God has chosen, and the things which are not, to bring to nothing the things that are, that no flesh should glory in His presence.
>
> Verse 23-29

Christ suffering on a Roman cross may seem to be a very foolish thing. If we see it with *pseukikos*, or *sarkikos* natural preference we will ask, "What kind of grace and glory is this?" But if we see with *pneumatikos* knowledge we see the power of God and His wisdom; (1Co 1:18) then we know the love of God for hopeless humanity. God in His wisdom gives knowledge to the world also, but it plays a trick on men without Love. And those who think they're the most wise are the actually the most foolish of all if they miss Love. (1Co 13:1-3)

Samaritan woman: Are you greater than Father Jacob who gave us this well?

Jesus: [You know not what you say.] I am here! I draw living water from MY Father's well and freely give to you...and you will never thirst again if you will drink of it.

Samaritan woman: Really? And why are you talking to me anyway? You're a man and I'm a woman. Right?? Never mind that you're from Judah. Don't they teach manners in Judah?

Jesus: [Oh? Really?]...But do you think you really know the mind of God concerning a man and a woman?

Samaritan woman: Why are you talking to me about GOD? You worship in Jerusalem; our fathers worshipped right here ...on this mountain.

Jesus: But God is seeking people just like you...[Even a Samaritan, unsaved, adulteress]...to worship Him in spirit and in truth.

Most Christians are far too horizontally attached to the world (oriented by an autonomous human nature) when it comes to knowledge, or preferences, or people— especially ourselves; this is a major stumbling stone. (Is 8:14; 1Pe 2:8) What do we really know about ourselves? What do we *want* to know about ourselves?

I remember so well, the pop culture of the 70's—and maybe it's this way with every generation—when we desperately wanted to "discover who we are", and some devised dangerous ways and means to do that, not the least of which was hard, psychedelic drugs and incredible promiscuity.

> A fool has no delight in understanding, But in expressing his own heart.
>
> Proverbs 18:2

Only a foolish person tries to discover himself in his own heart, for it truly is a bottomless pit of deception and wickedness. (Je 17:9) We can never discover who we are outside of Christ because outside of him we actually have no identity, (Mt 7:21-23) and if we ever think we have, it only turns out to be a trick; i.e. a game I think I'm winning but I'm actually losing. So I have a higher score than you, and I'm very happy; only problem is we're playing golf—not a foolish game at all—but I am indeed a foolish person if I'm trying to discover myself via myself and natural preference. (2Co 10:12b)

I could spend a lifetime climbing a ladder that actually leads downward, not upward, and when I get to where I'm going the Word of God is ringing in my ears: I have chosen the foolish things of the world to confound the "wisdom" of your preferences...even your old pick-up truck, your chainsaw, your girlfriend, the old oak tree out back, a bottle of beer and a cigarette at Joe's Bar & Grill, a sentimental song, a little white lie, a big business partner with a tantalizing deal, et al...

God has chosen natural preferences to confound the knowledge of the lost—those who refuse His love—in the hope that they will finally arrive at the end of themselves and come to Him.

We must grow in knowledge,
but above all
we must grow in grace, and in knowledge of
Love,
lest we become
knowledgeable fools.

6

Love That Forgives

Without Him We are so arrogant, so confident and sure of our selves, so puffed up with knowledge; but where is Love ...and where is forgiveness? It is where Love was crucified!

There was a thief who was crucified with Jesus, and he taunted him and challenged him to come down from the cross and save them both. He was using *pseukikos* knowledge in a desperate attempt to save his life, and it totally failed. Only Love does not fail.

There was *another* thief who had been crucified just before Jesus was. As he hung there in agony—naked, bloody, beaten to within an inch of his life, and in totally, hopeless despair—he was astonished at what a wretched person he had become, that he would end up being...crucified! With tear filled eyes he looked down upon another cross lying on the ground. And the Roman soldiers threw Jesus upon it; held his arms and legs as they drove the rusty spikes through his hands and feet. Jesus' body trembled with trauma. But then the thief heard those amazing words from his trembling lips:

"Father...forgive... them... for they know not...
what they do."
No greater words
can express God's willingness to forgive.
And no greater love
has any man than this.

Even in the throes of crucifixion this thief recognized *Love That Forgives* and he knew in his heart it was his only hope; he was absolutely right. The next words from his mouth were: "Lord, remember me when you come into your kingdom." In that instant—before the he could ever speak all the words of the sentence (Is 65:24)— God gave him a new heart, and Loved him, and this hopeless, helpless, crucified thief received that love. Jesus responded, even as they raised his own Cross, "Assuredly I say to you, *today* you will be with me in Paradise!" (Lu 23:42-43)

Without a doubt the soul of this thief was the last one saved before Christ's death; he is probably the very last Old Testament saint. What might that mean? It just might mean that he was the first one to enter into Heaven, right behind Jesus. (Mt 20:16; Mk 10:31; Lu 13:30)

I can see it now: The Father and all the angels standing at Heaven's entrance—"The Pearly Gates"— trumpets sounding the victory, cheering and applauding their approach. Jesus steps out of the clouds, and "the thief that stole Heaven" is at his side with a huge smile on his face; millions of Old Testament saints liberated from "Paradise" (Ps 68:18; Ep 4:8) are following Jesus and "a crucified thief" right into the "third heaven" (2Co 12:2)... How amazing is that picture of Love? Try to imagine the rejoicing among the angels. (Lu 15:7-10) And what is all this rejoicing all about? Love that forgives!

When we look to God's Son on the Cross we may see many things, but two things we cannot miss: God's love, and forgiveness that would not be possible without it.

A well-known psychiatrist was heard to say, "If I just had a pill for forgiveness, and the guilt associated with it, 75% of our mental hospitals would be out of business."

Knowledge can never deal with guilt;
only Love can do that.

Samaritan woman: OK! Give me a drink of your "living water"...I'll take it!

Jesus: Good! Now, go and bring your husband; I want to give him a drink of this water also.

Samaritan woman: I don't have a husband...

Jesus: Actually I know that...I also know you've had five husbands, and you're living with one who is NOT your husband. Not that I approve, but that kind of knowledge really doesn't interest me...Bring the one your living with.

Samaritan woman: Wow! Sir, are you a prophet, or what??

Jesus: Yes, and more; I am The Christ—Messiah—I am God, the one who created you, I am you're forgiveness, I will wash you in my blood, take away all your sin; I will give you eternal life—living water! Now...what do you seek to know; is it reality? Or do you want knowledge that will puff you up like "a piece of bread"? "For by means of a whorish woman a man is brought to a piece of bread: and the adulteress will hunt for the precious life." (Pr 6:26) Do you think you will find what you need in "knowledge"; that you will win the right man with your wit? Or could it be that the precious life you seek is in me? Which do you prefer? Shall I come to you with a rod of correction, or shall I come to you with Love—the more excellent way? (1Cor 4:19,21)

If we seek knowledge without Him, we will find
nothing.
If we seek of Him, we will find Him,
And we thus find Love, the most excellent way.

6

Love Will Not Make A Golden Calf

Now I plead with you, brethren, by the name of our Lord
Jesus Christ, that you all speak the same thing, and
[that] there be no divisions among you, but [that] you
be perfectly joined together in the same mind and in the
same judgment.

1 Corinthians 1:10

Pr. Tom Schaller:

Our Greater Grace staff has been together now for
over three years and I don't know of one time when
any one of us has gotten angry and caused serious
division; not one time have we had a disagreement
and somebody went stomping away into their own
little corner of self interest, or some personal want
or need. We lift our eyes above "Jim," or "Joe," or
"John," or "Peggy Sue," or any preference we might
have; even Greater Grace World Outreach, the
person setting next to us, a particular Pastor, or
anything, or anyone. All of us do all things with
Love and *pneumatikos* knowledge operating in our
midst.

It's like Love passing knowledge: In a footrace
between two runners—Love and Knowledge—Love
over takes and passes Knowledge, and is the *winner*
every time because Love edifies; it is the more
excellent way. It is the winning way that forgives,
and touches our hearts, and ever reveals the nature
of Christ to everyone around us.

I often think of how tricky life can be; how no degree of knowledge can ever deliver me from the power of death.

The late Ted Kennedy (1932-2009), a world-renowned, U.S. Senator from Massachusetts for 46 years, a prominent member of a wealthy, well known family, recently died of brain cancer. He accomplished many wonderful works in his lifetime; he was always a beloved and very influential person. But all his good works, all the fame and fortune of the Kennedy family, all his powerful, political friends, and the latest, greatest medicine and doctors and modern medical technology that money could buy, could not save his life...Only God's love could ever do that, and we certainly do believe he is now with God, not because of his wonderful works, for they are as nothing without Love, but by receiving Love by grace through faith, not of works lest any man should boast. (Ep 2:8-9)

Even we as believers often search for vain things and want a golden calf to worship. But we pray that the Spirit of God will impress upon our hearts that we live in a realm where we can see the invisible. We can see Christ—others cannot see him, but we can—and we can hear truth—others cannot hear it, but we can—and we can know the true value of things; the chainsaw, the old oak tree, our friends and family, whatever we love—it doesn't matter what it is, we all have a propensity for things that can steal our hearts...And we know the scientist and his evolutionary theories have a power of persuasion that can blind us to God's love if we will entertain that kind of knowledge.

God is saying: "Come! Come to me; come to the God of Abraham, Isaac, and Jacob; come to me who brought you out of Egypt; come to me who fed you in the wilderness of Sinai, come to me who sent the Prophets to you; come to me who sent His only begotten Son to save you; come to me who will give to you the Holy Spirit and eternal life; come to me and I will give you rest, and I will make your life immeasurably valuable beyond anything you could ever ask or think."

Knowledge of self can cause much grief and despair in life if we don't absolutely take authority over it in our heart. Therefore I know nothing against myself, and I judge nothing before its time, but I wait upon the Lord to bring all things to light in a proper perspective. (1Co 4:4-5)

Clara Barton (1821-1912) was a pioneer American teacher, a civil war nurse, and a great humanitarian, famous as founder of the American Red Cross. She was once reminded by someone of an especially cruel thing that was done to her many years ago but Miss Barton seemed not to recall it at all and looked at the informer as though to ask, "What are you talking about?"

And her friend asked, "Don't you remember?"

"No!" she quickly replied, "I distinctly remember forgetting it."

Maybe you have knowledge of yourself—or someone else—that isn't edifying. Don't let unedifying, corrupt knowledge come out or your mouth, only that which is good for edification (Ep 4:29)...Love edifies! If you know something about your teenager, or your wife, or your husband, instead of sending them on a condemnation trip, try Loving them.

> He who covers a transgression seeks Love, but he who repeats a matter separates friends.
>
> Proverbs 17:9

Hatred stirs up strife, but Love covers all sins.

Proverbs 10:12

Don't hold grudges; never let knowledge usurp authority over Love. You cannot be free and happy if you harbor grudges; put them away, collect postage stamps, or coins, or coca-cola cans, but not grudges. Better yet, collect Love! "Just Let God Love You" every chance you get. It will see you through, it will forgive you, it will forgive others, it will even forgive your enemies, and it will edify you and bless you, and never, ever fail you.

Aaron will make a golden calf for us if we want. While Moses is away, we need something to worship, and we do have the knowledge of how to make a golden calf just like the one back in Egypt if need be. So we could make ourselves an idol, bow down to it, and worship away our life until there's nothing left in us. But Love will not make us a golden calf, no matter how much we know. Love does not listen to *pseukikos* or *sarkikos* knowledge because it's knowledge that is twisted, distorted, and feeds us with deceptive concepts in human understanding. We know the truth—that God has chosen the foolish things of the world to confound the wise; the weak things of the world to confound the things that are mighty; the base things of the world, and things that are despised, and things that are not to bring to nothing the things that are; that no flesh shall glory in his presence. (1Co 1:26-29)

Knowledge puffs us up,
Love edifies us,
and liberates us.

Chapter 7
— God's House Is A Man —

Love Is Stronger Than Our Heart

Romans 1 through 8 gives us an amazing panorama of humanity's progression from hopeless *unbelieving* to Love *indwelling,* in a wonderful, inseparable, indivisible relationship with our Creator.

> Because, although they knew God, they did not glorify Him as God, nor were thankful, but became futile in their thoughts, and their foolish hearts were darkened.
>
> Romans 1:21

In Chapter 1 we see the immoral unbeliever [Ro 1:29-32]—and we do see a lot of unbelief and immorality all around us but God is ever seeking these to come to Him, to worship Him in spirit and in truth, and to receive His love, the cure for every sin-sick soul.

> But to those who are self-seeking and do not obey the truth, but obey unrighteousness--indignation and wrath, tribulation and anguish, on every soul of man who does evil, of the Jew first and also of the Greek; but glory, honor, and peace to everyone who works what is good, to the Jew first and also to the Greek. For there is no partiality with God.
>
> Romans 2:8-11

In Chapter 2 we see the Jew and the Greek philosopher who is morally right but totally lost, [Ro 2:11-16] and we do also see a lot of philosophic, pseudo spirituality in the world. But no philosophy can do what Love can.

Or is He the God of the Jews only? Is He not also the God of the Gentiles? Yes, of the Gentiles also, since there is one God who will justify the circumcised by faith and the uncircumcised through faith. Do we then make void the law through faith? Certainly not! On the contrary, we establish the law.

Romans 3:29-31

In Chapter 3 we see the religious Jew, also lost even though circumcised in his flesh, (Ro 3:1-3) for all have sinned, all have fallen short of the glory of God, (Ro 3:23) and circumcision must go beyond the flesh to the very heart of unbelief. (Ro 2:28-29) The love of God is like His Word—a two-edged (He 4:12) sword well able to circumcise the old heart and replace it with the new. (Ez 36:26)

In our own lives we know how easy it is to turn inward—be introspective, analytical, and religious; we know of the frailty of our bodies, we know in our relationships with one another—and even with God— how quickly we question and doubt Love.

Now to him who works, the wages are not counted as grace but as debt. But to him who does not work but believes on Him who justifies the ungodly, his faith is accounted for righteousness...

Romans 4:4-5

In Chapter 4 we have this amazing message from God: Sinners that we are, in our weakest state of unbelief, without any works whatsoever, we have been justified and declared righteous by God the instant we believe on Him. Meaning, God decided, in himself, before the foundation of the world, that you and I (we who believe) would be loved with an unconditional Love that would never fail and never change. He does this for the sake of His own glory by revealing, in time and space, His true nature to all of His creation. In so doing, even our failing will work to His advantage. He will be glorified before the entire universe—all of mankind, angels, devils and demons, even birds and animals and trees; on the earth, under the earth, above the earth, and in all of Heaven itself. Creation will ultimately know without question that He is God, and God is Love. (Ps 98:8; Is 55:12; Ro 8:22, 14:11, 1Jn 4:8,16)

In all of nature we see that God is powerful and wise. But now we see beyond nature to the work of His only begotten Son, and we know that God is Love..."For God so loved the world that He gave His only begotten Son, that whoever believes in Him should not perish but have everlasting life." (Jn 3:16)

My heart always condemns me, but Love is immeasurably stronger than any heart. There is therefore now, NO CONDEMNATION for ME !

7

God's Immeasurable House

Thus says the Lord: "Heaven is my throne, and earth is my footstool. Where is the house that you will build me? And where is the place of my rest?

Isaiah 66:1

Pr. Tom Schaller:

God is saying, "Where is my house? Is it in Lhasa, Tibet, the Capitol of Buddhism; is it in Madras, India, Hinduism; is it in Rome, Italy, Catholicism; is it in Geneva, Switzerland, Protestantism; is it in Mecca, Saudi Arabia, Islam? Where is my house? It's in a man; I have a man for my house."

And why is a man different from a building, a river, a mountain, or a religion? A man was lost—spiritually dead, cut-off from God's love—but if he believes he has a spirit that is made alive and is now in communion with an Immeasurable Dimension. Houses can be measured but this man cannot be measured; rivers and even the universe can be measured but this man cannot be measured because he is indwelt by Love, who cannot be measured.

We love to look out over the ocean because our eye does not see an end to it and God has created us for eternity. (Ec 3:11) When we look to the heavens and the stars we love it because our eyes are not stopped; the spirit in a man is amazed and enthralled as it searches the deep things of God. (1 Co 2:10-12)

183

That God has created us to be absolutely forgiven is also exciting to our spirits because they naturally hunger and thirst for eternal things. Tell me something that stirs my heart and touches my spirit; I have an affinity for spiritual things because they reveal immeasurable love.

> For as by one man's disobedience many were made sinners, so also by one Man's obedience many will be made righteous.
>
> Romans 5:19

In Chapter 5 of Romans we see only two men in the world: a dead man and a living man—the dead, first Adam and the born-again, living, second Adam who will never again be the first Adam...Never again will God see me as He did the first Adam who became a sinner.

> For the wages of sin is death, but the gift of God is eternal life in Christ Jesus our Lord.
>
> Romans 6:23

Abraham actually had two sons: Ishmael and Isaac, but Ishmael was the son of Hagar, his wife Sarah's Egyptian maidservant. [Ge 16:1-3] And God said to Abraham: "Take now your son, your only son Isaac, whom you love, and go to the land of Moriah, and offer him there as a burnt offering on one of the mountains of which I shall tell you." [Ge 22:2]

This is truly a *finished-work* scripture—the only one where we know Abraham via that which touches and excites our spirit—Love, grace, forgiveness, and the eternal of God. But we are strange people; even though we may know these things about our justification without works in Chapter 3, explained more thoroughly in Chapter 4, defined precisely in Chapter 5, and is our victory in Chapter 6, yet we see the craziness of our own flesh in Chapter 7, and that is still in us.

Pr. Tom Schaller:

Have you felt it recently; have you lived in your flesh lately? In one way I hope you have, that you might be refreshed in this writing. And if you have not, hallelujah, you are refreshed.

But we have felt the flesh—our fallen nature—and the actual physical frailty of it; the ripple affect of it when the mind is out of focus; the heart that becomes cold; the spirit that seems not to be moving—even dead; the time consciousness of today, tomorrow, my past; the dimensions of the world, 1 mile, or 2, or 1 inch or 2, or when I say, "I almost made it", or "I have failed very much." These are quantitative words like, "very much", "almost", "nearly", "just about"; or "I love you, just a little." But Love is not *quantitative* it is *qualitative*.

I remember so well when my son, Justin, was just a child. I asked him how much he loved me, and he said, "Two pieces, Dad!" meaning two pieces of candy because sometimes, when he was a good boy, he would get one piece of candy—two would be like over-the-top, a good boy! So I was blessed to hear, "Two pieces..." because I know it really meant, I love you very, very much, and I also know quantitative words are the best we can do in our flesh.

God asks, "Where is my house?" If you measure Solomon's temple you can count the steps; you can measure Noah's ark, you can evaluate a quantity of gold or silver, and you can even quantify love if it's human love. But where is my house? It is in a man; it's in a man who can comprehend the eternal, a man who can be loved unconditionally; and forgiven, and forgiven, and forgiven, and forgiven, until it breaks his heart and he bows his head and says:

"Thank you, Lord.
I Love you!
And I worship you
because you are not a man who is measuring;
you are God,
who is immeasurable."

A few years ago I went to South Korea to visit with Pastor Steve DeVries and our ministry there. Pastor Jeff and Nancy Phelps also came from China with fourteen precious Chinese disciples from their ministry. I was deeply touched just by their presence, and I knew immediately that they were all very much in tune with us. It was as though I had known their Pastor all my life. His eyes would light up with every verse we quoted. I learned that he had translated over five years of our messages into Chinese. When I heard that I knew Pastor Jeff and Nancy had been mightily used of God to reach these people. But how could it happen? Only because we communicate the immeasurable; we say God loves us— not just as in a cliché, but knowing His love in a personal way—and we declare with conviction, "It is possible to reach China!" knowing it actually is because we cannot measure what God will do in His great love wherewith he loves us. (Ep 2:4, 3:20)

Pastor Jeff sang a song about China and we had to pass the Kleenex around. Somebody shouted, "Today South Korea, tomorrow China!" meaning, we're all praying that, by God's grace, Christian ministry in China shall be every bit as powerful as it is in South Korea.

We are all very excited about what God is doing in these nations as the Gospel is being preached. Men and women came to me in tears to say, "We listen to all your messages on the Internet and we are loving every one of them with our whole heart." I was so edified by their Love for the Word.

At a 6:30 AM prayer meeting we were filled with the Holy Spirit as He came to bear us up in our weakness, not knowing what prayers to offer, or even how to offer them worthily. Throughout our conference we felt His presence and anointing upon every meeting. (Ro 8:26)

Who is sufficient for these things? But what happened to us when we believed? We were translated from the kingdom of darkness into the kingdom of His dear son; (Co 1:13) we actually entered into the eternal. And what happened to our hearts? They became eternal, something far greater than mere flesh and blood. What has happened to us? Yes, we're sinners and, as such, sometimes don't know which end is up, but when we're alone with the Lord for just a little while we look inward and operate from the new heart of the inner man, in the Holy Spirit. Yes, we stumble and sometimes we even say something that isn't edifying to someone; in a certain state of mind we all have that potential, but we have another potential. We are His house; we abide with Him and we bear much fruit. (Jn 15:5)

"Where is my house?" God asks.
And maybe we say, "We're busy right now."
But God asks again, "Where is my house?"
It is a man and that man is Jesus Christ, and he is in us.

> *He is the head of us,*
> *the Body;*
> *we abide in Him*
> *and He in us*
> *We are*
> *...the Temple of the Holy Spirit.*

7

Love Does Not Condemn

For we know that the law is spiritual: but I am carnal, sold under sin. For what I am doing, I do not understand. For what I will to do, that I do not practice; but what I hate, that I do. If, then, I do what I will not to do, I agree with the law that [it is] good. But now, [it is] no longer I who do it, but sin that dwells in me. For I know that in me (that is, in my flesh) nothing good dwells; for to will is present with me, but [how] to perform what is good I do not find. For the good that I will [to do], I do not do; but the evil I will not [to do], that I practice. Now if I do what I will not [to do], it is no longer I who do it, but sin that dwells in me. I find then a law, that evil is present with me, the one who wills to do good. For I delight in the law of God according to the inward man. But I see another law in my members, warring against the law of my mind, and bringing me into captivity to the law of sin which is in my members. O wretched man that I am! Who will deliver me from this body of death? I thank God--through Jesus Christ our Lord! So then, with the mind I myself serve the law of God, but with the flesh the law of sin.

Romans 7:14-25

There is therefore now no condemnation to those who are in Christ Jesus, who do not walk according to the flesh, but according to the Spirit.

Romans 8:1

In Chapter 7 we find the word, "I" (Greek, *ego*: the personal pronoun, I; joined to a verb means, having force and/or emphasis.) used 370 times in the New Testament (KJV); 8 times in Romans 7 and 0 times in Romans 8). In Chapter 8 we find the word "Spirit" (Greek, *pneuma*: the

Holy Spirit of God; i.e. a moving of air, a wind.) used 385 times in the New Testament (KJV); 0 times in Romans 7 and 22 in Romans 8. The transition from the first verse of Chapter 7, emphasizing self-condemnation, guilt, and insecurity, to the last verse of Chapter 8, emphasizing the Holy Spirit and eternal security, speaks to us of the total renovation of the soul of the sinner by the pure power of Love.

Paul's heart would surely condemn him, but God's love is greater than Paul's heart. (1Jn 3:20) God, the Holy Spirit, will always comfort us; God, the Holy Spirit, will pray with us; God, the Holy Spirit, will lead us in faith, God, the Holy Spirit, will make His Word known to us; God, the Holy Spirit, will build us into His Body; we are God's house, and here is no better housekeeper than God, the Holy Spirit.

Jesus Christ is seated at the right hand of the Father in eternity where he lives forever more, to continually, constantly make intercession for us. (He 7:25) And the Holy Spirit of God indwells every fiber of our being, for we are His Temple (1Co 6:19) and He prayerfully makes intercession for us with every beat of our heart—even the old heart. (Ro 8:26-27)

When God says, "I love you!" (Je 31:3) its with Love that is immeasurable, and that's the mind of God, the Holy Spirit. When God says, "I have saved you." (Ro 5:10, 10:3) don't question it for one second because it is immeasurable Love that has saved you. And when you have failed many, many times over, yet the Comforter will Love you and comfort you, and make intercession for you. (Jn 16:7)

> And we know that all things work together for good to those who love God, to those who are the called according to His purpose.
>
> Romans 8:28

The Holy Spirit is saying:

I know; it doesn't look good, but I am God; and I am in you; you are my house, and I want to show you my mind—there are 3 things I want you to know.

#1) Eternal perspective:
Not human viewpoint from a time-space perspective,
but from eternity—
with an eternal value system.

#2) Understanding:
I want to give you understanding,
with divine viewpoint.

#3) Love Inseparable:
Not love that has its source in the emotions,
but Love that has its source in who I AM.

7

#1 – Love's Eternal Perspective

Elisha's servant trembled at the enemy host surrounding them. But Elisha prayed that God would open the servant's eyes and show him the reality of the situation, and immediately he saw the mountain full of horses, and chariots of fire all around them, many more in number than the enemy. (2Kg 6:15-17)

God, the Holy Spirit, wants every believer to know that the miracle producing power of eternal Love is just as available to you and I as it was to Paul and Elisha. It is a part of our inheritance from the moment we first receive the Love he pours out to us from eternity through the cross of Jesus Christ. (Ro 5:5) Love in us sees great and mighty things that we know not of. (Je 33:3)

Now, wisdom is the principle thing; therefore, get wisdom, but with all our getting, let's be sure to get understanding (Pr 4:7)—divine perspective, discernment and instruction in the application of knowledge. If we practice eternal perspective we will understand what the will of God is, (Ep 5:14) we will know that all things are for our sakes, (2Co 4:15) we will know that His thoughts toward us are always good and never evil, to give us hope and a future, (Je 29:11) because He will lead us and guide us with loving-kindness. (Je 31:3) Then we will understand that we are called beyond the woes of this world to the wonders of eternity.

Jesus warns us that in the world we will have tribulation, even as he did. (Jn 14:2, 16:33) But he encourages us with assurance that he is preparing a place for us in eternity, and to store up treasures in Heaven because where our treasure is there will our hearts be also. (Mt 6:21; Lu 12:34) And not only that, but we also glory in tribulations, knowing that tribulation produces perseverance; and perseverance, character; and character, hope; and hope does not disappoint, because the love of God has been poured out in our hearts by the Holy Spirit who was given to us. (Ro 5:3-5)

If there's anything we need in the midst of the tribulation of the world it's to have our heart fixed on the eternal value system, not a temporal one, "while we do not look at the things which are seen, but at the things which are not seen, for the things which are seen, are temporary, but the things which are not seen, are eternal." (2Co 4:18)

And "treasures in Heaven" consist of much more than rewards for good deeds, they are the development of an eternal relationship with Him through trials of faith in time and space. In Heaven we will have a new name, (Re 3:12) and a "white stone" with a new name written on it, which nobody understands but the one who receives it—and of course, Jesus, the one who gives it. (Re 2:17) I do believe that the new name on this white stone is a trophy of Love's victory over the greatest of our weaknesses and temptations. We will not remember that we ever had them because He will have wiped away any remembrance of any sin. (Re 7:17; 21:4) But when we look at that beautiful, white stone with our secret name on it we will know that, in Christ, we won a great victory over the sin that did so easily beset us (He 12:1) in our time-space, faith experience. And we will know that His great Love for us was the key to that victory.

Wisdom is:
the application of knowledge.
Understanding is
the application of Wisdom.
Love is:
their link.

7

#2—Love's Understanding

Paul prayed—and wrote from his prison cell to the Church in Ephesus—that God would give to them a spirit of wisdom and revelation—insight into spiritual mysteries and secrets—in an intimate knowledge of Him. Paul desires that the eyes of their heart be flooded with spiritual light, that they might know and understand the hope to which God calls them, and how rich is His glorious inheritance in the saints; that they might know and understand the immeasurable greatness of His power toward all who believe. (Ep 1:17-19)

Yes, Romans 7 is real, but so is Romans 8; there is now, therefore no condemnation. God is saying in this Chapter: "Let me Love you, let me be the one that will carry you, let me be the one that will uphold you, and show you my Love."

Jesus is saying, "He who has my commandments and keeps them, it is he who Loves me. And he who Loves me will be Loved by my Father, and I will Love him and manifest myself to him...If anyone Loves me, he will keep my word; and my Father will Love him, and we will come to him and make Our home with him." (Jn 14:21, 23)

Do you see it? That's what life is actually all about—Love, and about God who is Love, about God making His home in us, living with us and through us as we walk with Him in the Great Commandment. (Mt 22:37-39) But we can't understand it unless we have people that really fail, people that have really sinned, people that are really wrong, people that are really weak, and people that are really disappointed with themselves and

193

how they handle life. We just don't know how to manage it with the wisdom of the world—we need wisdom from above. We can't understand it with human love alone, we absolutely need His love—the key to all understanding.

> For whom He foreknew, He also predestined to be conformed to the image of His Son, that He might be the firstborn among many brethren.
>
> Romans 8:29

From Divine perspective there are no surprises. He foreknew me and predestinated me to be conformed to the image of his Son. Meaning there is a precious promise in this scripture that guarantees unconditionally that ultimately I will be just like his Son. Because those whom He foreknew—of whom He knew and loved beforehand—he destined from the beginning to be molded into the image of His Son and to share inwardly his likeness, that Jesus Christ might be the firstborn of many. This is one very, very, very, precious promise!

> Moreover whom He predestined, these He also called; whom He called, these He also justified; and whom He justified, these He also glorified.
>
> Verse 30

This has already happened for us! This is how it is written; like it's already over, finished, a done deal before time began. And now God tells us that we're his house; that He predetermined, preplanned, and made it all possible through he death of His Son; that you and I, now and forever, without any question whatsoever, will be the continual object of His love—no holds barred, no doubt about it, no questions asked, no matter who you are, or what has happened to you, or what you have gone through recently it simply can never be challenged or changed. God has called you to Himself, He has also justified you—acquitted you and made you righteous, automatically putting you in a right standing with

Himself; and He has glorified you—raised you up to a Heavenly dignity and state of being...simply because you *believe*.

> What then shall we say to these things? If God is for us, who can be against us?
>
> Verse 31

Pr. Tom Schaller:

Who can be my foe if God is on my side? (Ps 118:7; He 13:6) If God is for us everything and everyone is also for us; if we have been predetermined to be like him; if we are absolute objects of His love; if that love cannot ever be questioned, what can we say of these things?

God's Word is, "If God is for us who can be against us?"

I answer: "I will tell you who's against me, Lord, My self-consciousness."

And God will say, "I crucified that!"

I will say, "My sin is against me."

And God will say, "I took care of that on the Cross."

I could say my own design and nature as a person is against me but God will say, "It is not a question; I am for you! Nobody, nothing—and that includes you—can change it forever!"

What can we say to these things? Thank You, Jesus! And, Amen!

> He who did not spare His own Son, but delivered him up for us all, how shall He not with him also freely give us all things?
>
> Verse 32

I think we are made to be touched by the spirit; I think we are made to have fellowship in the mystical; I think we are made to look up into eternity and comprehend that there is something much bigger than ourselves; I think it is amazing that we can have a vision for China, or Korea, or Baltimore, and can be so edified by His great love for us. I think it is amazing that even in our subconscious mind we can be cleansed and feel the power and the authority of Love in our own spirit. If He did not withhold His own Son, but offered him up for our sins, He will surely not break this precious promise made to every one of us who believes on Him.

Three Hebrew boys, Shadrach, Meshach, and Abedn-Nego, were "called on the carpet" by King Nebuchadnezzar because they refused to bow down and worship his golden image. (Da 3:13) They were told that unless they did so—on the spot—they would immediately be thrown into a burning, fiery furnace. But they said, "If Our God is able to deliver us from the furnace, He will deliver us out of your hand, O king. But if not, be it known to you, that we will not serve your gods, or worship your image in any way whatsoever! (Dn 3:17-18) Do whatever you want, O King; we have no concern, for there is something eternal about us—all of us—all who believe—we are made for the Spirit, we are His house, and you cannot burn that house down no matter how hot you make that furnace."

And indeed the king did have them thrown into the furnace and turned it up seven times hotter than normal—until it even fried those tending the furnace—but the Hebrew boys were totally cool in there, and when the king looked in to see how they were doing, they weren't even sweating. Their hands were bound before they were thrown in, but now their bonds had been burned off without ever harming them one iota. And to the King's astonishment, there was a fourth person in the furnace with them; (vv. 24-25) the pre-incarnate Christ himself was there to encourage them and cheer them on. When they let them out there was not a hair on their head that was singed, nor was there even any smell of smoke on their clothes. (v. 27)

Nebuchadnezzar said, "Blessed be the God of Shadrach, Meshach, and Abed-Nego, who sent His Angel and delivered His servants who trusted in Him, and they have frustrated the king's word, and yielded their bodies, that they should not serve nor worship any god except their own God! Therefore I make a decree that any people, nation, or language which speaks anything amiss against the God of Shadrach, Meshach, and Abed-Nego shall be cut in pieces, and their houses shall be made an ash heap; because there is no other God who can deliver like this."

Then the king *promoted* Shadrach, Meshach, and Abed-Nego". (vv 28-30)

The Spirit intercedes, "Believe me! Please!"
The flesh says, "No! No! No! Not me!"
But there is the cry and the call of God's Love saying, "Believe me, surrender, worship me, trust me, follow me, and I will show you great things that you know not of; not only when you go to Heaven, but even in this lifetime. I will groan within you, I will pray through you, I will build you up in your inner person, and I will reveal my Son to you. And you will reveal him to the kings of the earth." (1Kg 4:34; 2Ch 9:23; Ps 138:4; Ez 27:33)

We may know it all,
but we understand only what faith puts into
practice,
and Love sees us through.

7

#3 – Love

> Who shall bring a charge against God's elect? It is God
> who justifies. Who is he who condemns? It is Christ
> who died, and furthermore is also risen, who is even
> at the right hand of God, who also makes intercession
> for us. Who shall separate us from the love of Christ?
> Shall tribulation, or distress, or persecution, or famine,
> or nakedness, or peril, or sword?
>
> Romans 8:33-35

Will tribulation or trouble separate me from His love?
I realize that we have troubles; I have a sin nature also,
and I realize how life can be very challenging—we all
do—but we meet challenges at the door and bring them
before the Him saying, "Lord I have tribulation, distress,
famine, persecution, nakedness, peril of the sword..."
and these are real words that some brothers and sisters
everywhere really have to deal with daily. But we cast
all our cares upon Him, knowing that He cares for us,
(1Pe 5:7) we listen to what he has to say, and we hear from
the depths of our heart a still, small voice (1Kg 19:12) saying,
"Nothing can separate you from the Spirit of my love?"

> As it is written: "For Your sake we are killed all day long;
> we are accounted as sheep for the slaughter. Nay, in all
> these things we are more than conquerors through him
> that loved us."
>
> Verses 36-37

Were Jews going to the slaughter for His sake yet?
Yes, they were, and we cannot question sovereign grace.
What do I think of that? I think it is senseless for us
to be divisive; it is senseless to take up a cause that is

not the amazing cause of knowing and comprehending His love, because we are more than conquerors through him that loved us; therefore, in all these things, we can well afford to lose in order to gain.

> For I am persuaded, that neither death, nor life, nor angels, nor principalities, nor powers, nor things present, nor things to come, nor height, nor depth, nor any other creature, shall be able to separate us from the love of God, which is in Christ Jesus our Lord.
>
> Verse 38-39

We all have lost loved ones; we all know that that's like. But even death is not a problem—not even if it's our own. For we are .p.e.r.s.u.a.d.e.d.

Nebuchadnezzar! Bring it on! Turn it up 7 times...14 times...a squillion times! Give it your best shot because we will take it to the Cross, where you will learn—if you haven't already— that Love is inseparable; nothing can separate us from His love.

Nebuchadnezzar said, "I thought we put three men in that furnace."

They answered, "True, O King; three!"

"But look! I see four; [Can't you count?] And one of them is shining like he's the Son of God!"

Sooner or later that must be the nature of our experience, because it absolutely is the nature of Love, to reveal Him in our fiery trials, and what is freely given to us in Him.

And there are things that are sometimes even worse than death. Even so there is a spirit that searches the inner parts of the soul of man, (Pr 20:27) the deep things of God, (1 Co 2:11) and the deep calls unto the deep (Ps 42:7)—the heart of God and the heart of man became one in the Spirit of Love—then there is this confession by the apostle Paul, and by all of us: I am persuaded—I am persuaded...I know in my heart—not even death can separate this love.

And the Lord will say, "Where is my house?"

And there is a man on death row saying, "Not even death...I am persuaded, that neither death, nor life, nor angels, nor principalities, nor powers, nor things present, nor things to come, nor height, nor depth, nor any other creature, shall be able to separate me from your love, God."

And God will say, "There it is! This is my house! That's where I live. I live in a man and a woman; I live in a man in prison; I live in a woman in China; I live in a man in South Korea; I live in a woman in Thailand; I live in a man in India; I live in a woman in Baltimore, MD, in our State, in our Nation; in their prayers; I love where I live and nothing is ever going to separate me from my house. That's a promise! Wild horses couldn't drag me away!"

And it is not a program of works, it is absolutely what God is doing in our hearts—drawing us closer to Him in an ever more intimate relationship.

Pr. Tom Schaller:

I believe in our Bible College, that God will continue to give us the kind of ministry that will disciple men and women of the Spirit.

And yes, we will often say, "I this... I that... I will... I won't... I... Me, I, myself!" But then we will say, "God this... The Holy Spirit that... Jesus... Jesus... Jesus!" Because Love teaches us, Love leads us, Love constrains us, Love loves us, and Love persuades us that nothing can separate us from Love.

Paul is saying, "I am persuaded... I am— p.e.r.s.u.a.d.e.d."

But Paul, look at you; dirty clothes, living in a little shack, no certain dwelling place, address unknown... in much patience, in tribulations, in needs, in distresses, in much patience, in tribulations, in needs, in distresses, in stripes, in imprisonments, in tumults, in labors, in sleeplessness, in fasting (1Co 6:4,5)

Paul says, "Yes, but I am persuaded by Love that I must write these words; that many years from now they will still be read by precious people who need to know of Love's power."

Of course we don't really know how much Paul knew about the future, but we are sure it was he who was caught up into the third heaven and saw many things that he was not permitted to speak of. (2Co 12:2) We do know that this is the life we've been called to live. It's in our hearts, it's in our music, it's in our teaching, it's handing out tracts, driving a nail, sweeping the floor, changing the baby, preaching the Gospel, giving thanks to God, praying, always and ever praying and praising God, always knowing that life or death, no height, no depth, no creature shall ever be able to separate us from the love of God that is in Christ Jesus our Lord. Nothing! Never!

I was glad when the Father, Son, and Spirit said,
"Let us go into the house of the Lord."
for I am persuaded that means—
YOU and I.

Chapter 8
— Upstairs Faith —

The Love Song

The Song of Songs, which is Solomon's.

Song of Songs 1:1

Jewish tradition interprets Song of Songs as an allegory of God's love for Israel; our early Church Fathers interpret it as an allegory of Christ's love for his Bride, the Church; in any case its theme reveals another facet of God's nature of love: it's faith factor. Without faith it is impossible to please Him, [He 11:6] for he that comes to God must believe that He is, and that He rewards those who seek him. [He 11:6]

Song of Songs is a poetic mystery of mysteries, and isn't God's love also? It's interesting that we find it at the center of the Bible—at the very heart of Sacred Scripture; where else would we find such blessed subject matter? I personally enjoy this book, because it continually helps me to understand and appreciate the walk of faith that Love calls us to.

Solomon wrote one thousand and five songs [1Kg 4:32] but this is his Song of Songs, far and away his most excellent. In the same sense that the heart of the Tabernacle was called the Holy of Holies, and the Lord Jesus Christ is called the King of Kings and the Lord of Lords, [Re 19:16] this book is called the Song of Songs. Preceded by the book of Ecclesiastes—an exposition on "vanity of vanities"—it is like an antithesis of it. Ecclesiastes speaks of a life of wandering; Song of Songs speaks of a life of rest from wandering. Ecclesiastes speaks of seeking all things under the sun; Song of Songs speaks of seeking all things in Christ. Ecclesiastes teaches us that we can never find satisfaction in life by knowledge alone; Song of Songs teaches us that we can find the satisfaction we long for through Love.

Solomon is mentioned in the first line; his reign was one of peace in Israel and he is the king who is the figure of the Christ, seated above in all his glorious triumph over the Cross—Satan, sin, and death itself—the battle is over, peace reigns under the Prince of Peace. The Shulamite, his bride to be, is a poor, uneducated, common, country maiden, a figure of the Church as the Bride of Christ, which may mean either the individual or the collective Body of Christ, but it may be preferable to see her as an individual because the maiden's longing is indicative of the individual's exercise of spirit rather than that of the corporate Church.

Our life in time and space is like living on the first floor of a two-story building. The first floor is the world of phenomena—life and death, material things, real life experiences, joy, happiness, sadness, etc—all existing things. It is a world where we are conscious; reacting, responding, enjoying, hating, suffering, happy, and sad, in relationships with other people, having many wants and needs, but we never do seem to get the whole picture—we don't know what's upstairs. We can imagine that maybe there is an upstairs but that's all we really know because the second floor is a spiritual realm. And the human spirit is behind everything we experience in life, but we're not able to rightly interpret its thoughts in a natural state of existence on the first floor because spiritual things are inaccessible to the natural man. (1Co 2:14) On the first floor we live life as we know it naturally, but in our heart of hearts we're always looking for the staircase. We want to know why; we want to know where we're going; and we also would like to know where we came from. We have many questions that need answers and we sense that if we could somehow access this second floor we just might be enlightened.

Song of Songs is truly the *Love* Song of *Love* Songs.

> *Whether we're aware of it or not,*
> *we're somehow ever searching for a mystical*
> *stairway*
> *to the second floor of life.*

8

The Faith Factor

[The Shulamite] Let him kiss me with the kisses of his
mouth—for your love is better than wine. Because of the
fragrance of your good ointments, your name is ointment
poured forth; therefore the virgins love you. Draw me
away! [The Daughters of Jerusalem] We will run after
you. [The Shulamite] The king has brought me into his
chambers. [The Daughters of Jerusalem] We will be glad
and rejoice in you. We will remember your love more than
wine. [The Shulamite] Rightly do they love you.

Song of Songs 1:2-4

A great King has come out of the city on his chariot to
meet and fall in love with a simple, Shulamite, country
maiden. This is a picture of us; simple, common people
living in a world we know relatively little about, and the
King comes to us and wins our hearts with his love. He
is also a lead player in the poetry of Song of Songs. He
is coming to his Bride, but then going away, and she is
longing for him because of the way he touches her, the
way he loves her, the way he cares about her, and what
happens in her heart when he is initiating his heart of
love to her.

She is attracted to him as we are also. Somehow
Love is that way; men have a natural affinity for it. His
Disciples are as Daughters of Jerusalem who love their
King and minister his Love to her. And as they do she
can readily understands their Love for him.

Pr. Tom Schaller:

I want to encourage you in understanding, knowing,
and believing that your life has a dimension that is

much larger than the first floor permits. Actually there is a person that lives on both floors. It may seem like he has gone away and left you, but he's only calling you; drawing you up to the second floor.

> No one has ascended to Heaven but He who came down from Heaven, that is, the Son of Man who is in Heaven.
>
> John 3:13

But we can see him...we can see him! We [believers] are the only people on the planet that have been equipped to see him; born of God to see the Son of God. He said, "A little while longer and the world will see me no more, but you will see me..." (Jn 14:19) He also said, "With fervent desire I have desired to eat this Passover with you before I suffer; for I say to you, I will no longer eat of it until it is fulfilled in the kingdom of God." (Lu 22:16) But by faith his disciples did eat bread again with him; and by faith we also eat bread with him.

I think there could be no more fervent desire and prayer in the heart of God's people than this: "Lord could I go to the second floor? Could I sit at your feet and listen? Will you minister to me? Could you answer my questions? Even if you don't answer them my way—on my level—could you...?

> *Could you... show me your mind so that,*
> *as I live on life's first floor,*
> *I can endure your suffering?*
> *I can live by faith?*
> *I can live my life with authority from you?*
> *Because, behind my life,*
> *there must be a reason that is beyond reason."*

This life abounds with first floor reasoning—and the world loves it—but reason on the first floor will not get you *off* the first floor. It cannot bring you from life to eternal life, and it cannot bring you from love in a human way to Love, which is divine.

God saw that the wickedness of man was great in the earth...*that every imagination of his heart was only evil continually,* (Ge 6:5) [interpreted from the Hebrew meaning, a formulated matrix of thought—i.e. a basket constantly and continually filled with evil]. And that means you and me! And we may imagine that, as we get older, the evil will become less. Not so! Ask any old man or old woman and they will tell you, "Evil is right there in me continually from my childhood to my death!" Evil is in the very heart of natural man; his matrix of thought definitely is not one of faith.

But on the first floor, faith actually is part of the phenomena, for God has put a measure of faith in every man; (Ro 12:3) people have faith here on the first floor, but faith in and of itself cannot save anyone; only saving faith, faith in a Savior—living faith in the resurrected, living, Lord Jesus Christ—can do that. It must be that God leads us to that mystical, staircase that is His Son; (Ge 28:12-15) it must be Him who lifts us up to where we can have access to, and abide in the whole house—with Him.

Death and suffering is a first floor phenomenon that is often very difficult to understand. Why do so many godly, righteous people suffer? Why do so many good things happen to bad people? And why do so many bad things happen to good people? Well, we're all only human, but when we meet people that live in the whole house we sense that there's a mystery in them, like in Song of Songs.

Pr. Tom Schaller:

The late D. James Kennedy (1930-2007), pastor and founder of the Coral Ridge Presbyterian Church, Fort Lauderdale, FL, —also a renowned televangelist— taught Christians to share their faith by asking two disarmingly simple questions: #1 Are you sure you're going to Heaven when you die? #2 Upon what do you base your certainty?

Pastor Kennedy was strongly affected in the 1950s by Dr. Donald Grey Barnhouse on his Christian radio, "Bible Study Hour." Dr. Barnhouse persuaded Kennedy that he should embrace the Christian faith, which he did. And he went to the seminary and became a Pastor. Early years were difficult for Kennedy; but he learned door-to-door evangelism from close friend, Kennedy Smart, and he used it faithfully. Ultimately a consistent application of the two-question formula he personally developed helped his Church grow to a membership of 10,000, the largest of his denomination. Pastor Kennedy never quit his habit of weeknight door-to-door visitation. He was one who discovered the stairway to the second floor and never took his eyes off it until the angels came to take him to the third floor.

Pastor Jerry Falwell (1933-2007), another great leader in the Church in our nation, recently passed on to eternity and Heaven.

And our beloved Billy Graham also is living out his last years in poor health.

At this writing I am 75 years young, and I must say, I wouldn't have it any other way—even if I could. Life has been good and bad, but the last thing I would ever want is to have to do it all over again. I really do believe "Jesus wept." (Jn 11:35) because Lazarus was already in Heaven... and it broke Jesus' heart to have to call him back to Planet Earth—the last thing his friend would want and the last thing a friend would ask of one he Loved—to leave the eternal bliss of the third floor, and go all the way back to the first. Love was the only thing that could have ever enabled him to go back, and surely the only thing that enabled Jesus to ask him.

Now I love to ski—I mean, really—and I really can ski. I was in Park City, Utah in 1982, having such a great time that I gave very serious consideration to taking up residence right there and just becoming a "ski bum". I was thinking that maybe God could use me to evangelize the slopes of Snowbird and Alta, which for me, at that time, was nothing less than Heaven on Earth.

I was waiting for a bus to the airport and a flight back to NY, thinking I would deliberately just miss that bus (like I used to miss the school bus when I was a teenager). Then I heard it—God's voice knocking at the door of my heart—almost audibly! He called my name, and softly said three things I shall never forget: #1 "I love you very much. #2 "Get on that bus." And #3 "I have a mountain for you in Heaven."

I immediately threw my suitcase on the bed, dumped the dresser drawers into it, grabbed my skis, and was out the door as the bus was pulling up to the motel. I got on it! That same week, back in NY, the Spirit of God led me to The Bible Speaks ministries, in Lenox, MA, the ministry that introduced me to the second floor life. And I don't know when the day will come that I'm called up to the third floor—cause I really do feel great—but when it comes, I'm not just going home, I'm going skiing!

We understand death far and away better than most because:

We live in the whole house
knowing we have eternal life
And we will indeed
...never die

209

8

Love's Voice

I am dark, but lovely, O daughters of Jerusalem, like the tents of Kedar, Like the curtains of Solomon. Do not look upon me, because I am dark, because the sun has tanned me. My mother's sons were angry with me; they made me the keeper of the vineyards, but my own vineyard I have not kept.

Song of Songs 1:5-6

"I am dark," says the Shulamite to the daughters of Jerusalem. "...Do not look at me; I was once beautiful but the sun has tanned me—nature has taken its toll on my life—and its not pretty; I have many responsibilities that I don't even want and I feel the pressure of them every day; I have no life of my own."

Have you or I ever felt that way? Absolutely! We all feel the pressures of every day life. The system and even our own families are relentless in their demands upon our every resource. Welcome to the wonderful world of life on the first floor. Is there another way?

[The Shulamite] The voice of my beloved! Behold, he comes leaping upon the mountains, skipping upon the hills.

Song Of Songs 2:8

Suddenly she hears his voice, and he comes to her leaping upon the mountains, skipping upon the hills. (SS 2:8) He comes right down to the first floor; he handles the mountains and hills of life's tough times with ease. Our problems are no problem for him; he can handle the cancer, he can handle the heartache, he can handle the pain, he can handle the loneliness, he can handle

210

the disappointment, he can handle the divided heart, and he can even handle the grave. My heart is divided at times, and I hate that. How can it be that my heart is so divided? My eye must be single; (Mt 6:22; Lk 11:34) I want my eye to be single!

But, behold!! The voice of my Beloved—he comes to me—I hear his voice saying, "Take up your bed and walk!" I hear his voice saying, "Lazarus! Come forth!" I hear his voice saying, "Give me the five loaves and the two fish, and I will pray." I hear his voice saying, "Pray for Peter in jail; for I am God, I am the God of the prison. I am the great, I Am!"

Pr. Tom Schaller:

He is the ultimate reality of the mystical staircase we search for in our hearts. Only by faith can we see it, but he initiates to us, he skips upon the hills and leaps over the mountains, as though to say, "I know what the first floor is like, I know you have tribulation there—I understand—but look, I am the King, even of gravity itself. I'm the stairway up; come to me; trust me, have faith in me, don't be afraid, I will never, never leave you nor forsake you; ...*we will do this together.*

I shall never forget it: On a certain day I was spiritually worn to a frazzle (not to get into any details). But Pastor Schaller and I were walking together as we were leaving the chapel and we happened upon a person who was obviously hurting. We talked with him, and encouraged him, and hurried on. I knew Pastor was in a bit of a hurry to get to an appointment; and he said to me, "Pastor Ron, could you just go back an pray with him?" I said, "Sure!"—though, still a bit preoccupied with my own personal concerns, I really wondered if I could handle it. But then Pastor stopped; our eyes met, he hesitated, and said, "Let's do it together, Pastor Ron." And we did; but I saw his faith and sensitivity in that instant, and I was touched by Love. This kind of faith and discernment can only come from a second floor lifestyle, and, you can take it from me, our Pastor definitely has that!

> My beloved spoke, and said to me: "Rise up, my love, my fair one, and come away."
>
> Verse 10

"I'm only a car mechanic. Look at my hands; all gnarly, and arms with grease up to my elbows. I don't even know what you're talking about! 'Come away!' What's that supposed to mean?"

The heart is a deceitful matrix of thought that excludes second floor life:

"I'm a mother with five kids; been changing diapers all day, cooking, and cleaning. I don't know what that means. How can that happen for me? No! I live on the first floor; that's my life, that's the way it is down here and nothing can change it! I can't escape; nothing's moving my heart. Sorry, not interested; I don't even know what the heck you're talking about, and right now, I don't even really care."

But we care! Because there's enough of the Holy Spirit—the wholeness of His person in us—to cause us to hear his voice saying, "Calm down. Please, listen to me. I walk in the midst of the candlesticks, I show up in the night seasons, I leap over your mountains and skip upon your hills, I knock at the door of your Laodicean, human heart, (Re 3:14-22) I'm the one that lives in your body, and I'm asking you to live by faith—not by sight. Then I will fill you with my Spirit; then I will draw the veil back, and you will see me, and you will know the great truth that I Love you, and that will set you free from every care of the world." (Jn 8:32)

> Behold, he calls me up to the second floor
> where I have peace that passes all understanding
> for Love is...
> the Prince of Peace.

Pr. Tom Schaller:

The Lord is in His holy temple, the Lord's throne is in Heaven, His eyes behold us, His eyelids test the sons of men. (Ps 11:4)

It often seems like God is not looking at me—like He shuts His eyes to me. And I'm down here on the first floor crying out, "God, I'm in trouble down here! God, I'm hurting; do you know it? God, can you hear me way up there?" And it seems He's like a father who dozed off watching TV.

But God does not slumber or sleep. (Ps 121:4) God tests us with closed eyelids but His voice can be heard and He says, "This is what I've called you to. Yes, I did put you on the first floor, but I have also called you to be seated above in Heavenly places. (Ep 2:6) I have called you to hear what I have to say to you. And I will reveal to those who fear me, that this fear is the beginning of wisdom. (Ps 111:10; Pr 1:7, 9:10) I will show you great and mighty things you know not of (Je 33:3) and open this world up to you. I will show you the stairway to the second floor, and you will know the truth and the truth will make you free indeed. (Jn 8:32, 36) And, no; I will never, ever leave you nor forsake you, but I will be totally *invisible* to you because I want you to listen for my voice...*by faith.*"

> [The Shulamite] I sleep, but my heart is awake; it is the voice of my beloved! He knocks [saying] Open for me, my sister, my love, my dove, my perfect one..."
>
> Song of Songs 5:2a

What is it that knocks? I thought it was the hand that does the knocking, but it says a voice is knocking. I'm sleeping and his voice is knocking. I think that when I go to church God is knocking with His voice saying, "Awake, thou that sleepest (Ep 5:14) and follow me." But I'm sleeping, I've put off my clothes, I've put on my pajamas,

I have my cup of warm milk right here by my bed, and my Teddy bear; I'm all tucked-in already! So often it is in those moments of comfort that God's voice is knocking at the door of your heart. And He will say, "What do you want? Are you after me? Are you hungry after me? I want to show you some things; don't worry about your sleep, I want to give you real rest; I want to remove those shackles from your feet, and I want to deliver you from your bondage to sin. I want to show you the person who is the door:" (Jn10:7) the messenger of the covenant, (Mal 3:1) the beginning of the creation of God, (Mk 10:6) the answer to our every question—the way, the truth and the life, (Jn 14:6), the Alpha and the Omega—the beginning and the end of history, (Re 1:8, 1:11; 21:6; 22:13) and Love will lead you to the stairway to the second floor." (Jn 1:51)

He is the person that has changed our lives; by his faith we now walk in the newness of life. (Ro 6:5; Ga 6:20) Our hearts burn within us as we walk and talk with him, (Lu 24:32) and we say, "God is good, God is gracious, God is great, God is amazing; His loving-kindness is better than life." (Ps 63:3) "...Let him kiss me with the kisses of his mouth for his love is better than wine." (SS 1:1)

Natural ways and means to experience joy in my life cannot be likened to the kisses of life beyond the first floor; the best wine the world has to offer is as mere water by comparison. His love lifts me up to where my imagination and my heart can be stirred up in the faith.

Love's voice has brought me
beyond the structure of religion
to worship God who is
beyond eternity.

8

Love's Call

His voice comes to us from outside the box—from Heaven: Come! Follow! I will make you a fisher of men! (Mt 4:19; Mk 1:17) Come unto me! Take my yoke upon you, for my yoke is easy, my burden is light, and you will find rest in the depths of your soul! (Mt 11:28-30) The Spirit and the Bride say, "Come! And take the water of life freely. (Re 22:17)

And the Shulamite did come to him; now she is resting—sleeping—the experience of the Cross has dealt with her sin and self consciousness, she is in sweet, spiritual love-repose, but her heart is wide awake, ever alert to the sound of his voice. She lives on the first floor where her outward person needs rest and peace, but her spirit soars on the second floor where she is fine-tuned to the clear sound of Love knocking at the door of her new heart, speaking to her with beautiful, encouraging words, fitly spoken as "apples of gold in pictures of silver". (Pr 25:11)

> ...He knocks, saying, "Open for me, my sister, my love, my dove, my perfect one; for my head is covered with dew, my locks with the drops of the night."
>
> Song of Songs 5:2b

Oh, that we might learn to let the Lord love us in spite of our frailty and failure. It must have excited her heart when she heard those words; and we should hear them also. Think of a man with godly initiation, loving a woman who has taken his heart. She is excited, her heart stops when he speaks, his words are as flaming arrows piercing her heart: Open to me my sister—flesh

215

of my flesh, bone of my bone— (Ge 2:23) my love, my dove, my undefiled, my sinless, my righteous, my redeemed, my justified; for my head is filled with dew (from being out in the early morning or late night when the water drops from the atmosphere and covers his head in the night)—and my locks with the drops of the night.

"Open to me" indicates that there is yet a deeper phase of her calling. "My sister" means I am of the royal family of God—I have the divine life; "my love" means she understands God's purpose; "my dove" means she is sealed with the Holy Spirit; "my undefiled" points to her holiness, purity, and dedication. But his locks soaked with "the drops of the night" takes us back to Gethsemane (Lu 22:44) where there is the suffering side of the Cross, as well as the redemption and deliverance side. And it may well mean that even her disciples, the "daughters of Jerusalem"—those who have been interested and excited about her relationship with the King—may abandon her as the Cross lays the axe to the very roots of natural life. Her co-crucifixion experience made her a river of life to many; now it may bring her to a place of shame, contempt, loss of position and influence, and even diminished opportunity to serve God, even as it did her lover when his Father turned his back and refused to look upon him in the hour of his deepest darkness. (Mt 27:46) Jesus was not only a servant, he was a suffering servant, "a man of sorrows and acquainted with grief" (Is 53:3) [At this stage of my personal life I think I'm just beginning to understand the real meaning of this verse.]

And she seems to hesitate with an excuse, as though to stall for time to think this one over for awhile.

> I have taken off my robe—must I put it on again? I have washed my feet-- must I soil them again?
>
> Verse 3

She was all tucked-in—cozy, warm, and comfortable—
at least for the moment. But aren't we all as we go about
our day-to-day business on the first floor, knowing the
work is finished (Jn 19:30) and grace is abundant. (Ro 5:17)
How well I remember those first days—even months—of
my walk with the Lord. I had such a sense of security
through saving grace. For the first time in my entire life
I was beginning to relax a bit; I could say, "Just letting
God Love me."

In her flesh, the Shulamite is not all that excited,
and may even have been somewhat annoyed, and with
good reason. In our first floor experience we also have
good reasons for not being available when he calls us
up to a new level of intimacy with him. We have lots of
worrisome, troubling things that wear us down, close our
eyes and lull us to sleep; many reasons, many excuses,
many distractions, many fears, many cares and woes,
many details of life—things we can talk about and think
about and muse over en ad infinitum if we don't just
"open" and let God love us right where we are, right
now. The Apostle saw this great truth when he wrote:
"Yet indeed I also count all things loss for the excellence
of the knowledge of Christ Jesus my Lord, for whom I
have suffered the loss of all things, and count them as
rubbish, that I may gain Christ." (Pp 3:8)

> My lover thrust his hand through the latch opening; my
> heart began to pound for him.

Verse 4

But her spirit is moved with desire to go to him at
all costs. He is at the door—standing outside, and as
he speaks his hand passes by a hole in the door; she
caught sight it. All she saw was his hand but it was
enough. This is like us also; in our first floor, everyday
life we may not always be seeing all of God but we often
do see a little of Him. We get a glimpse of his hand as it
passes by a hole in the door—some little thing plucks a

heartstring and gets our attention. A little miracle here, a big one there, answered prayers, healings, salvations, deliverance, situations and circumstances that defy natural explanation; these are little glimpses of his omnipotent hand—his presence in the details of every life— even at the heart's door.

I have his spoken Word, I have the moving of God, and it may not be great—i.e. God appearing to me like He did to Paul on the road of Damascus [Ac 9:3] —but something moves my heart, and I know it, I see it, and I say, *"That was all I needed to cause me to believe."*

It may be that when you read your Bible, something suddenly jumps off the page and gives you deeper understanding of truth; or the preacher said something from the pulpit, and new insight into the reality of God's nature of love is revealed to you; or someone you don't even know had a word in season for something you're going through; but you're encouraged and edified in Love that reveals him by faith, with all grace and mercy, in your weakness.

> I arose to open for my lover, and my hands dripped with myrrh, my fingers with flowing myrrh, on the handles of the lock.
>
> Verse 5

Encouragement empowers her to open the door; she is now ready to abandon every excuse, and go all the way with him.

Myrrh is a gum resin used as perfume and in the embalming process; it was the same gift the wise men brought to the Infant in Bethlehem, and it foreshadows his crucifixion death. Her hands are dripping with myrrh; it's as though she is suddenly holding in her hand the personal possession of her co-crucifixion with him; it's that real! It cannot be seen but the aroma of it cannot be missed; it fills the house—*both floors*; it is a picture of the first floor meeting the second, it is a picture of our total being—body, soul, and spirit—embracing the Cross. God gave us a nose that we would be able to sense something we cannot see—an aroma of myrrh or frankincense; and our new heart does have an innate ability to see the invisible when it senses Love at the door.

Have you ever felt like this? By pure faith, you reluctantly get out of bed and say, "OK, I'm up! I'm going to the door; He is there." Maybe it's just a prayer meeting or a Sunday morning service, but you've been up all night worrying about something; and it seems like you just fell asleep. Or it's Saturday morning; time for the outreach meeting, and it's very cold and the wind is blowing, but you don't even have to pray about it. You reach for the latch on the door and suddenly there's an amazing beautiful aroma of resurrection life flowing from hands that only want only to serve their Beloved. You can't see it but you somehow sense the reality of it in your heart; you're quickened. The deep is calling to the deep [Ps 42:7] and brings to your consciousness the remembrance of his death, burial, resurrection, and ascension. You know this is what life is really all about, you forget every other concern; the wind, the rain, the heat of the day, the cold of the night, [Ec 11:1-4]...whatever— the love of Christ keeps your heart focused on him—you begin to experience Love; and you open the door of your heart to receive it. And suddenly, the first floor and the second become one; you're ready to receive Love—for him, yourself, your neighbor, your enemy, if necessary— you're going forward in the plan and purpose of God to take His love into all the world

We cannot explain this faith to everyone—what we are seeing and hearing and believing—because we are praying to be filled with the invisible; the knowledge of his will in all wisdom and spiritual understanding; that we might walk worthy of him; that we might be fruitful in his name, and grow in grace and in knowledge of him; that we might be strengthened with all patience, and longsuffering with joy. (Co 1:9-11) We hear his voice knocking and we know we are called into something that is from God; it is the person of Jesus Christ, our King, our Beloved, and someday we will see him and know him face to face. My Beloved is mine; and I am his. (SS 2:16)

> I opened for my beloved, but my beloved had turned away and was gone. My heart leaped up when he spoke. I sought him, but I could not find him; I called him, but he gave me no answer.
>
> Verse 6

Pr. Tom Schaller:

She goes out in to the street and cries, "Where is he?" She cannot find him again...Again! O my! Where is he? Suddenly it's life as usual; life is real after all on any given day...and I'm looking around again and seeing what it's like to live on the first floor...Again! But I'm saying, "O, no! That is not hindering me at all. I have the Word, I have the faith, I have the Body of Christ, and I have the testimony of God on earth. O, no! I'm drawing near, I'm believing, I hear his voice skipping on the hills at every service. That is it! And I'm saying, "I am able! God has made me able! I am well able to get up and open the door of my heart to his love.

Love equips my heart with faith;
eyes to see him,
hands to serve him,
feet to walk with him

And I say all this because I believe most of us have a hunger for the life of faith in Christ to be drawn out of us; that it should not go unnoticed by us, that we would not be familiar with that reality.

But please do not live in a first floor, crystallized, Christian life:

"Yes, I'm a Christian; saved!"

"Yes, I read my Bible every day!"

"Yes, I pray every day!"

"Yes, I know we're living in the end times!"

"Yes, I know that doctrine!"

"Yes, I know all that!"

Yes, yes, yes, yes! But that's life on the first floor only—one-dimensional Christianity!

We cannot put "Who we are" in a box, and we cannot even begin to imagine who we are in Christ. (1Co 2:9) We can't explain it, but we can live it. We can say, "O, I see him!" "I'm OK!" "I believe!" "I know...I know." "His grace and mercy reaches as far as the East is from the West; the sky isn't high enough to contain him, and the ocean isn't deep enough to drown Love."

Also we are a poor people with an evil, divided heart; grumpy, strutting all around on the first floor, and asking, "Why did this happen to me?"

"I am dark from many hours in the scorching sun; I have many vineyards of others to keep, and I can't even keep my own—so many lives to care for that I can't even care for my own life the way I should."

But Jesus says, "I have an answer for that; I am God, I will lift you up, give you access to the whole house, and to reveal my Father to you in the process. I will reveal him to you, and you will have a testimony of him. This will set you free and you will be free indeed."

Come to me, my beloved.
Your problem isn't you,
it's just that you still live on the first floor.

Chapter 9
– Find The One Your Soul Loves –

Small Sin Stifles Great Love

Nowhere in the Bible do we find that we're called to salvation by grace through faith (Ep 2:8-9) so that our Christian experience might give us an excuse to "stop and smell the roses". God is not content to save us and just give us grace right there for the rest of our natural life. We are called to a pilgrimage—a journey of faith through this present world—that necessarily involves being on the move. Let us go forth therefore unto him without the camp, bearing his reproach. For here have we no continuing city, but we seek one to come. (He 13:13,14)

Sodom, Lot's hometown, was entirely corrupted by evil, immorality, and sexual perversion, (Ge 13:12-13) all of which was undoubtedly infecting him and his family. So much so that God sent a special envoy of angels from Heaven to evacuate Lot and his family, and destroy the city, including inhabitants. (Ge 19) The angles had to physically force the family to leave, (Ge 19:15-16) and they forbade them to look back as they went. When they were at a safe distance, fire and brimstone began to rain down upon the city and the area around it (including the city of Gomorrah). The roar of ruination was ringing in their ears when Lot's wife could no longer resist the temptation to take one last look, back at her beloved home; perhaps she was hoping to see some of her friends escaping with them. But she was instantly—on the spot—transformed into a solid pillar of salt. (Ge 19:24-26) What is the lesson in this? What is God thinking? He loved the family enough to send angels to deliver them, but one little mistake makes Lot a widower and his children, motherless?

But Lot and his family were in Sodom to be a testimony of God's love for the lost; instead they had fallen under its spell of "small sins" (Ge 19:20) which they actually believed did not offend God. But God absolutely is offended by every sin, no matter how small it may be. I cannot indulge in small sins if I know I've been forgiven much, for then I desire to Love much. (Lu 7:47)

C.H. Spurgeon:

Little sins are as mighty for mischief in their multitude, as if they were greater sins. Have you ever read the story of the locusts when they sweep through a land? I was reading but yesterday of a missionary who called all the people together when he heard that the locusts where coming up the valley; and kindling huge fires, they hoped to drive off the living stream. The locusts were but small; but it seemed as if the whole of the blazing fires were quenched—they marched over the dead and burning bodies of their comrades, and on they went, one living stream. Before them everything was green, like the Garden of Eden; behind them everything was dry and desert. The vines were barked, the trees had lost every leaf, and stretched their naked arms to the sky, as if winter had rent away their foliage. There was not then so much as a single blade of grass, or sprig upon the tree, that even a goat might have eaten. The locusts had done all this, and left utter devastation in their track. Why this? The locust is but a little thing! Ay, but in their number how mighty they become! Dread then a little sin, for it will be sure to multiply. It is not [but] one, it is many of these little sins. The plague of lice, or the plague of flies in Egypt, was perhaps the most terrible that the

Egyptians ever felt. Take care of those little insect sins, which may be your destruction. Surely, if you are led to feel them, and to groan under them, and to pray to God for deliverance from them, it may be said that in your preservation is the finger of God. But let these sins alone, let them increase and multiply, and your misery is near at hand. Listen not then to the evil voice of Satan when he cries, "Is it not a little one?" (Spurgeon: Park Street Pulpit; Sermon No. 248; Little Sins.)

It might seem to be a very small thing to disobey a divine directive; but *obedience* might just be a matter of life or death. The sin of Lot's wife seemed like a small one; but it was the one God chose to use as an example of salt that lost its savor, because of what it considered to be "small sins"? And what good is salt if it has lost its savor, but to be trampled under the feet of men? (Mt 5:13) Lot's wife became a prime example of how important it is to go forward—without ever looking back—in God's plan to remove us from the evil influence of immorality; to use us to manifest his great Love for a world of "small sins" that will certainly bring about its total destruction.

The people of Sodom and Gomorrah would blush at the immorality of this present world; even they, never imagined same-sex marriage. Many believe these things are one of the sure signs of the immanence of divine judgment on a global scale, even the time of *Jacob's trouble,* (Je 30:17)—*Great tribulation* as prophesied in the Book of Revelation.

Satan tries to convince me that it's only
...a small sin,
but God gave His only Son
to die for ALL my sin—
small and ALL.

9

Seeking Love

[The Shulamite] By night on my bed I sought the one
I love; I sought him, but I did not find him. "I will rise
now," [I said], "And go about the city; in the streets and
in the squares I will seek the one I love." I sought him,
but I did not find him. The watchmen who go about the
city found me; [I said], "Have you seen the one I love?"

Song of Songs 3:1-3

"Night" in the Hebrew is plural; the Shulamite has
sought him for many nights, and does not understand
why it is so, but her Beloved is capitalizing on her feelings
for him, to draw her out and into his plan and purpose.
She sought him in the bed and did not find him; she
sought him in the streets and in the squares and did
not find him; but we see the heart of a believer in her
seeking, and it is moving toward him—becoming ever
more intimate. This is a picture of us; by faith we move
forward in his plan; we move toward him, worshiping
him who we cannot see. She is not content to stay on
her bed and wait, and want, and wish; when she cannot
find him she goes seeking, and we who believe are ever
seeking him also, for the promise is: If you seek me you
will find me. (2Ch 15:2; Lu 11:9) And we worship as we go—
ministering wherever we go—asking, "Have you seen
him? Have you met him along the way? Do you know
where he can be found? Do you know him? Oh, he is the
one my soul loves! Do you know about him? If ever you
did you would understand why I search."

We carry the testimony of God and Love with us
wherever we go; we meet many who respond to it, for
he has put them in the way, and prepared the way—the

hearts—and many are encouraged in the faith. This is where we find him; not in our bed, but in going forward in his great plan and purpose to take the Gospel of His love into the highways and hedges of the world of the lost. (Mt 22:9-10; Lu 14:23) What better way could there be to send His love to the lost, than to send it in a soul he Loves? What wisdom this is?? Seeking him, but finding the lost, and him in the process. So often we think we minister him to people, but we find that he ministers to us through people—even the lost. We seek the one our soul loves, and we find him in the Loving of souls that are lost. For the Son of Man has come to seek and to save that which is lost. (Lu 19:10)

There are watchmen out in the world watching for you, and they will find you; they think they're not seeking anything, but their hearts actually are, because God is seeking them. (2Ch 16:9) But they find her—the Shulamite— who has a heart that is loaded with Love, and this love is contagious and spontaneous to save souls.

> *I was sought by those who did not ask for me;*
> *I was found by those who did not seek me,*
> *I said,*
> *"HERE I AM...! HERE I AM...!"*

> Scarcely had I passed by them, when I found the one I love. I held him and would not let him go, until I had brought him to the house of my mother, And into the chamber of her who conceived me.
>
> Verse 4

Here is an amazing mystery: She wasn't even aware of it, but her presence—the presence of Love in her— ministered to the watchmen; something happened to them—and maybe it did, or did not—but as soon as she passed by them she found him, the one her soul Loves.

So often this is what happens to us; in our daily activity there are many watchmen—people observing when we're not even aware of it—they're drawn to something even they can't explain, but we can. It is the one our soul Loves; it is his Love working in and through us. We are a tree of life, (Pr 11:30) a river of living water, (Jn 7:38) a living epistle known and read of all men, (2Co 3:2) and much of the time we're not even aware of it because, by faith, we're only seeking the one our soul Loves; that's our focus!

But sometimes "watchmen" are worldly; worldly wisdom, reasoning, and fear are as watchmen. *Reason* finds us seeking, so we reason for a season, but we pass on from it and into faith where we immediately find him. Or worldly *wisdom* finds us seeking, and we consider it for a season but we pass on from it also, and into the arms of him who our soul Loves. *"Fear of man"* finds us seeking and we're fearful for a season but we pass on from that too, and into faith where we find God who is Love, and He always gives us a victory. (1Co15:57)

The devil wants you to stop and look back at the life you left, like Lot's wife—and become a pile of salt that has lost its savor, to just blend into the dust of the earth where nobody will recognize you as children of Love. He wants you to stop and reason, or intellectualize, or talk, and talk, and talk, and talk…until talk lulls you to sleep; then he sends you nightmares about all your problems. He wants you to stop at your worry, stop at your family conflict, stop at your business problem, stop at your past, or your personality, *stop when you reach age 75*— to be mesmerized by all sorts of worldly cares and woes. But Love says, "If you pass by these problems you will find me; if you pass by it all, and just let me Love you, you'll find me waiting to be gracious." (Is 30:18-19)

Now that she has found him she does not want to let him go; she clings to his feet—the symbol of his very walk of faith in the world. She will bring him to her mother's house. And, if we consider the home of her mother to be the place of grace, then the chamber where she was conceived is the place of Love. She desires to forever possess his presence in the ambience of Love and the manifestation of Love, which is grace. In our relationship with our Beloved we soon discover one of Love's greatest lessons:

GRACE ← *is the only consciousness that can contain Him, who is... LOVE.*

> Not that I have already attained, or am already perfected; but I press on, that I may lay hold of that for which Christ Jesus has also laid hold of me. Brethren, I do not count myself to have apprehended; but one thing I do, forgetting those things that are behind, and reaching forward to those things that are ahead, I press toward the goal for the prize of the upward call of God in Christ Jesus.
>
> Philippians 3:12-14

The Apostle was doubtless a model of spiritual maturity, but he never stopped moving forward, for he was seeking the one his soul Loved.

The Lord says, "Come to me; pass the world by and you will find me." And the Bible echoes it off the walls of the world no less than six times... verbatim: "Whosoever shall seek to save his life shall lose it; and whosoever shall lose his life for my sake shall find it." (Mt 10:39, 16:25; Mk 8:35; Lu 9:24, 17:33; Jn 12:25) My life; what is that? The one whom my soul Loves; "For in him we live, and move, and have our being; as some of our own poets have said, 'For we are also his offspring.'" (Ac 17:28) And the problems may still be real but the peace of God that passes all understanding—or we might just say: Love—covers our hearts in the midst of the problems. (Pp 4:7)

We know Love never fails us; we know Love has a mind that thinks with doctrine, and it's very important that we pay attention to Love's thoughts in our heart. There is a mystery in Love that commands complete concentration.

Pr. Tom Schaller:

As I sat in my office alone; concentrating and meditating—and I paced the floor, and knelt in prayer, and submitted my soul to Love—then the Lord spoke to me with this verse:

> And Moses said to the people, "Do not be afraid. Stand still, and see the salvation of the Lord, which He will accomplish for you today. For the Egyptians whom you see today, you shall see again no more forever.
>
> Exodus 14:13

I love this! When you see the Egyptians coming at you, stand still, see the salvation of God—pay attention, stop, look and listen, receive Love, see your salvation and you won't see the enemies of your soul any more... forever. There are enemies but in order for us to see them for what they are we really need to stop and pay attention to Love's thoughts concerning them. Our relationship with God is wonderful, as we know in our hearts that awesome, mystical fellowship of faith and peace that enables us to stand still in the presence of our enemies... Love them; relax and leave them to the Lord.

> The Lord will fight for you, and you shall hold your peace." And the Lord said to Moses, "Why do you cry to me? Tell the children of Israel to go forward.
>
> Verse 14-15

Now...lets move out; but I feel, and I hear in the background that idea of standing still, and even moving backwards—the whole idea of even being found alone and unarmed in the streets of a world of wickedness

> The watchmen who went about the city found me. They struck me, they wounded me; the keepers of the walls took my veil away from me.
>
> Song of Songs 5:7

To the watchmen she had been transformed in to a beautiful person, and they were actually puzzled over why she had ever lost her Beloved. They want to help her but their counsel of worldly wisdom makes her feel worse than ever—"they persecute the ones you have struck, and talk of the grief of those you have wounded." (Ps 69:26) If her Beloved was hidden from her they think it must be because she has somehow offended him, so they scold and berate her. She is naturally sensitive about her covering being violated and invaded, so the taking away of her veil is to add insult to her injury; now her failure is made public, and she would say, "Reproach has broken my heart, And I am full of heaviness; I looked for someone to take pity, but there was none; and for comforters, but I found none." (Ps 69:20)

The world at large always wants to get its hands on our faith; to rip away what we have, and expose our every imperfection for all to see—and they will often succeed but only in the measure that God wants to exercise and strengthen our hearts, for it is a faith that works by Love. (Gal 5:6) But if we move forward in our faith, if our heart has ears to hear the mind of the Holy Spirit, if we pay attention to the still, small, voice of Love, then we stand still in grace, we will see salvation's work in our life, and we will not see our enemies any more. That's the promise of God!

But there is sometimes a soul attachment like Lot's wife had, and it causes some to turn and take that one last look at a past which is loved more than the future, more than the mystery of the vision, more than the calling of God, and more than a walk of faith and devotion to Him. But these are things that are very important because we cannot move forward in the cause of Christ to make disciples in all nations of the world without them; we cannot get rid of our excess baggage unless we're moving forward. We must be moving forward in the narrow way that is Love. (Mt 7:13-14) And it's not a "broad" way but a wide way, it's not injury but healing, it's not failure but forgiveness, it's not worldly wisdom but doctrine it's not unbelief but faith, and it's not ourselves but God Himself.

It's as though I'm walking down Broadway in New York City and everywhere I look I see millions of people, all the bright lights, and the "broad" way—the way of the world. Many will be impressed, but I sense that something is missing. And it seems as though Broadway gets narrower with every step I take. Then I notice a little doorway down at the end of a back alley. And it's a little scary, but I'm drawn to it—I know not why—and I go there, put my hand on the knob, turn it, and it opens very easily, as though it was intended to be opened freely, by whosoever will. So I step through the doorway (Jn 10:7-9) just to take a look around, and ...Wow! ...WOW! ...There it is! Like, "I was blind but now I see"; the world of eternal Love opens on a horizonless realm that is wonderful beyond my wildest imagination. (1Co 2:9) I can hardly believe it! But I know I can never go back; this is what my heart has been searching for forever. I'm home at last. Hallelujah! Amen!

All of us have sinned, all of us failed, all of us are unworthy to even be breathing. We should not even be here, we should be off somewhere in a world of abstract living without definition, where we invent in our own minds whatever we want to believe; whatever we think, or whatever we can imagine in the hope that something will suit us, and it never really does. But, no! Now we're here and we're moving forward, serving a living God, in a new and a living way (He 10:20) that is energized by Love (2Co 5:14) in a world without beginning and without end.

A great price was paid to put us here:
the blood of the Son of God.
Christ on a cross,
opened the way for us to seek him;
to find him;
to be where we are—in him;
to pass by some of our craziness in the world;
and find him who our soul Loves.

9

Moving Forward—Following Love

Now it happened as they journeyed on the road, that
someone said to Him, "Lord, I will follow you wherever
you go." And Jesus said to him, "Foxes have holes and
birds of the air have nests, but the Son of Man has
nowhere to lay his head."

Luke 9:57-58

Jesus asks, "Can you live in a ghetto in the Philippines;
can you sleep in a train station in Ukraine, as many
have? ...Foxes have holes, and the birds of the air have
nests, but the Son of man has nowhere to lay his head.
(Mt 8:20; Lu 9:58) Can you do this?"

And what is our answer? "No; I cannot live like you
do; I cannot do that, I will follow you wherever you go,
but..."

Jesus says, "I love the idea of you moving forward
with me, but I don't want to give you a false impression.
If you do follow me, it will be me in you, and you will
follow me and find me, and you will do things you could
never have done on your own; indeed, you would not
even believe me if I told you what you will do. Would you
like to do that?"

Then He said to another, "Follow Me." But he said,
"Lord, let me first go and bury my father."

Verse 59

Jesus says, "C'mon; go forward with me."
And someone says, "I will, but first let me..."
And Jesus interrupts, "No! That's going backwards.
I want you to move forward with me—right now. Your

father or me; you decide... You must decide now, your father's funeral or me."

I love it that Jesus is not giving us the old "fast sell" routine, like a big contract document with gold and tinsel borders and nice, big letters at the top—then at the very end, lots of demonic, little letters that you need an electron microscope to read. No, no, no; he puts the bad news right up front in big, bold letters, then the *little letters* at the end:

> "...and you shall receive a hundredfold, and you shall inherit eternal life." (Mt 19:29; Mk 10:30)

Jesus is saying, "If you go home to bury your father you will not see me there; I'm on the move, I have something to do. 'I must work the works of him that sent me, while it is day: the night cometh, when no man can work.' (Jn 9:4) I want you to go forward with me—wash your hands of all these little impediments, shake the dust off your feet—pass by worldly distractions that meet you all along the way. I will not beat you; the world will beat you; I will Love you with no strings attached. Come with me! Let me put you to work with me; my work is easy, and you will find rest in the depths of your soul." (Mt 11:28-30)

> Jesus said unto him, "Let the dead bury their own their dead: but you go and preach the kingdom of God.'"
>
> Verse 60

Sometimes getting our priorities in the proper order is not easy in this world; they're different for every individual on a given day, and even when we think we finally have them right, they invariably change. The secret to getting them right every time is in seeking first the kingdom of God (Mt 6:33) at all times; or we might just say, "in seeking the one our soul Loves". Because when we find our Beloved, all other priorities find their proper place, or simply fade away into nothingness in the light of His glory.

Strange as it may seem to us, the flesh or the world just is not the right priority. The Love of God in our hearts, where we believe something beyond ourselves, is the right priority, and if we can get that right, our flesh will not be a problem. To get the first priority right is to automatically solve 99% of our other problems. And far and away the greatest problem the world has ever known—make no mistake about it—is in finding the one the soul Loves.

> And another also said, "Lord, I will follow you; but let me first go and bid them farewell who are at my house."
>
> Verse 61

"I will go with you; I will follow you—please, believe me—but let me go home and have a little, goodbye party. I need to let Mom & Dad know what I'm doing, and where I'll be...and who I'm with... You do understand that? Right??"

But Jesus is tough on relationships, because they're a weakness of the flesh that we all have problems with. Human love encourages sentimentality and soul attachments that abound in relationships, and very often impede our relationship with Love; then we easily become so focused upon wrong priorities that we have no time whatsoever to be a channel of charity.

It is entirely possible to get the first priority right by trusting God for all the others. He well understands our attachments to friends and loved ones, and is well able to manage and maintain them if we will let Him. He will, without a doubt, do a much better job than we ever could anyway.

There are many Godly men and women in our ministry who are seeking first the kingdom of God, serving God, and they are honoring their family relationships with their whole heart as they do so. But they're very careful to be lead of the Spirit, they're continually moving forward with God—following Him—they have His promise and Love's covering every step of the way, and it is amazing to see how things just seem to always fall into their proper place if He is in control.

There has been a number of times in my own life when I had to choose between a sentimental relationship with a family member or a friend, and following Jesus. Twenty years later those relationships are all exactly in order, and I am so glad I gave them to God and went on with Him.

> But Jesus said to him, "No one, having put his hand to the plow, and looking back, is fit for the kingdom of God."

Verse 62

When I was a boy my Grandfather took me with him one day to plow a field. This was back in the late 1930's when many farmers still used a single blade plow and a horse to prepare a field for planting. I walked along behind Grandpa and that old plow, and he made it look real easy. I wanted so much to take those reigns; I was sure I could do it! So I asked, "Grandpa, kin I try? Please, Grandpa?"

He smiled and said, "Sure ya can, Son!" and slung the reigns over my shoulder and stepped behind me.

"Giddyup, Prince!" (the horse's name) and he responded immediately. He was a huge animal; very strong and steady, yet gentle. Yes; gentle strength. I was surprised at how easy it was; Prince was doing all the work; all I had to do was hang-on and steer around a little stick or stone here or there. And I thought I was doing great, but when we got to the end of the field I looked back to admire my work. I was astonished at the crookedness of the row; it was all over the place. Grandpa didn't say a word as I just stood there looking back with my mouth wide open... but he had that little grin.

"Grandpa!" I said. "How did ya make your rows so straight?"

"Son; ya see that rock away out there at the end of the field?

"You mean the big one stickin up...with a little one right beside it?"

"Yep; that's the one. Now set your eyes on that rock—don't look up, don't look down, don't look sideways—steer your plow right at that rock, Son. Do it now!"

"Grandpa, should I look back to see how I'm doin sometimes?"

"No! Just do what I said, Son."

So I did what Grandpa said; And I didn't look back till I got to the end of the row; then I did...and, "Wow weeeee! Did I do that row straight, or what, Grandpa?"

"Yep! Ya did it, Son! Good job! Well done! Now lets finish the job. Back to work now!"

"Ok, Grandpa! Kin I do some more?"

"Yup! Go forward, Son. Just go forward now! Let's get it done."

Fix your eyes upon the Rock of your salvation—the one your soul loves—don't look back no matter what; if you do you're not up to it as far as seeking the Kingdom of God is concerned, because you're focused on all the little sticks and stones, and birds, and bees, and this and that all along the way. These are like details of life and sentimental attachments that we're always worried about—trying to steer around—and they just make a mess out of the plan of God if we let them. I'm not saying we should be careless about details, and certainly not loved ones, but I am saying that, over the course, we cannot afford to let them distract us and discourage us from God's plan and purpose. Relax! Rejoice! God is the "Prince" of peace. He is very strong—with a gentle strength. He does all the work, we just stay focused on the Rock; go forward and get the job done.

And we're forgetting the things that are behind, pressing towards the mark, for the prize of the high calling of God in Christ. (Pp 3:14) We make straight lines of faith in Him all the way to Heaven, "for so an entrance will be supplied to us abundantly into the everlasting kingdom of our Lord and Savior Jesus Christ." (2Pe 1:11)

We move forward plowing the fields of the world,
for a harvest of souls.
And we have our eyes firmly fixed on the Rock—
The one our soul loves.

Chapter 10
— The Wonder Of Love —

Wonder Is Wonderful

We are people who need to see the wonder of Love—the wonder of His person, His work, and the reality of our heavenly home.

I love watching, listening to, and thinking about the minds of little children, and I envy them sometimes—but not really so much—their *childishness*, no; but their *childlikeness*, yes—their wonderment about things, and especially the things of God.

> For God so loved the world that He gave His only begotten Son, that whoever believes in Him should not perish but have everlasting life.
>
> John 3:16

"God so loved the world" is something we desperately need to know with our whole heart. No other verse in the Bible reveals the character and nature of God—that He is Love [1Jn 4:8,16]—as this one does. And as we think about it, we would like it to grip our hearts and affect our lives in such a way that we are totally wonderstruck every time we hear it.

Pr. Tom Schaller:

One writer says, "Wonder is that possession of the mind that enchants the emotions while never surrendering reason." This is a very good definition; it lends itself perfectly to our feelings about—the

239

wonder of—His love for the world; it is very real to us, and our emotions love it.

When I was a child I would sometimes watch a Bugs Bunny cartoon and it was fascinating to me, but Bugs Bunny is not reality; I was always aware that it was only "make believe". But sometimes I see something real that deeply affects me and I internalize it, because it's emotionally enchanting to me, yet it is not contradictory to reason; this is truly a wonder. As I'm much older now, I've noticed that wonder is that part, or the function of my soul, that refreshes and excites me; I get excited when I discover something that is simultaneously fantastic and real.

Most adults are not so easily deceived, but children are; they're amazed, and they wonder at an optical illusion or a "magic" trick. And isn't it wonderful to watch children experience wonder? I think our faith refreshes us with wonder over and over again. When we really understand something for the first time, or when something totally new is suddenly brought to our attention, or when we see an awesome work of God in nature. Then there is always a feeling of wonder in our heart; we actually long for that *sensation* in our soul.

Christ is himself called "Wonderful", [Is 9:6] and in Isaiah 28, God's work is a strange work—it is wonderful—and even if it's told to a man he does not believe it. In Isaiah 53:1, we find the question: Who has believed our report?

> *"God so loved the world,*
> *that He gave his only begotten Son..."*
> *the most wonderful statement*
> *ever made.*

Pr. Tom Schaller:

Recently I read a philosophical discussion about relativity, absoluteness, and truth, wherein the writer said, "truth has a belly-button". Now, that is an interesting statement. *Truth* was born in human flesh—and I thought, "What?? How can this be? Can we believe it?" This statement is wonderful to me! That we can be removed from the philosophical, Pandora's box in such a way as to be amazed by a statement like this...is wonderful! We are amazed that God loves us so much that He came to this planet as one of us, in Christ, and lived a sinless life that qualified him before God, The Father, to die in our place on a Roman Cross. Wow! I have to stop right there and wonder at this amazing thing: *Truth* has a "belly-button." How wonderful is that?

God said to Job, "Where were you when I laid the foundations of the earth and the heavens, and angels sang?" (Jb 38:7)

Our very first sight of Heaven will be wonderfully beyond our imagination.
That wonder will put a new song in our heart, and it will be
#1 on the "Heavenly Hit Parade" (Re 14:3)
...forever.

10

The Ten Wonders of Love

There are many things in a time-space, universe that cannot be explained by its physics and philosophy of life, but we experience them every day, and they are very real and amazing. I want to share ten that I call: *The Ten Wonders of Love:*

#1   The Wonder of Nature

Pr. Tom Schaller:

There is an Alaskan bird that migrates annually, 4,000 miles across the Pacific Ocean to Hawaii. God has somehow built an automatic homing device into this little creature's body that calls it and directs it precisely to its destination. If it deviates a fraction of a degree it will die because, as it begins its migration, it has only enough fat stored up to provide the energy it needs to cross the water, and if it misses the islands it cannot swim. But God created it with all the necessary elements of life that we're witness to every day. Another bird migrates from Chile all the way to Canada.

And we say, "Can you tell me again, about the beautiful monarch butterflies?" And there are thousands of illustrations we could use, all of which fill us with wonder about God's creation in nature. Have you ever wondered why God does such things? Why doesn't He somehow let us know exactly how it is that a simple, little bird can accomplish something with ease that would challenge even you or I to the utmost, even if we have a compass? But it is to stir up wonder in our very heart—a homing device in and of itself that draws us, points the way, and guides us via the shortest possible route to Him who our soul Loves; even though we cannot see him, and must walk by faith. Only a God who is Love could have the wisdom that would create a universe filled with all the wonders of nature that we marvel at every day; wonders that draw us to Him in a beautiful, wonderful way.

#2   The Wonder of Mankind

I love to be around people to observe, and interact, and share ideas and concepts about most anything, to listen to them and laugh with them. The love of Christ constrains me (2Co 5:14) and equips me to take the Gospel into all the World, but it's wonder that *energizes* and *encourages* me.

Don't we love children; ever learning and growing in life? Full of wonder themselves, they are a wonder to one and all. Made in the image of God; it must be that even we—His children—are a wonder to Him as He observes every detail of our lives; our decisions, our likes and dislikes, our antics and humor, our joy and sorrow; and He loves us with a Love that is the greatest wonder of all. (Je 31:3)

> I will praise you, for I am fearfully and wonderfully made; Marvelous are your works, and that my soul knows very well.
>
> Psalm 139:14

> What is man that you would be mindful of him, or the son of man that you would visit him? For you have made him a little lower than the angels, and have crowned him with glory and honor.
>
> Psalm 8:4-5

Pr. Tom Schaller:

We would even go a step further than the psalmist and say, "Not only is man visited by God, but God became as we are—a man!"
"Wonderful! Wonder of wonders!"
"What? Say it again!"
"Yes, God became a man."
"Why??"
"For God so loved what he created that He could not just stand by and watch it destroy itself. He became a literal part of it; He came to Planet Earth—to us—with a desperate desire to save us from our sin nature, which has destined us to perish."

Why?
Because each and every one of us is His personal,
unique, one-of-a-kind,
masterpiece of creation!
And we are absolutely
irreplaceable.

Isn't it interesting that humans are found only on this planet; that it's only here on this Earth that we have life—complicated, complex, intelligent life—and not only life but *moral* life with a spirit and a soul, intelligence, emotions, a conscience, and a free volition; people asking the questions:
"Why? Where? Where are we going? What is it all about?"
"How is it that God so loved us, even in our spiritual blindness, and yet our greatness as being totally unique, that He became a man, and truth had a "belly-button??"
I know its humorous sounding but it isn't sacrilegious; it's honestly real and honestly true. Is this not amazing?

Pr. Tom Schaller:

Oh, Jesus, keep us young at heart, and thankful, and full of wonder at all that's around us, because we are weary in our soul and tired in our very constitution.

We so easily say, "I know! I know!" And, in desperation, just go to bed.

We say, "I know; I know all about it...but I'm so empty and lonely inside."

"I know; I know, but I'm getting older; crusty, and grumpy, and cranky. And I'm looking for some new thrill in my life, something to have a relationship with, something that will take my heart."

What you do have that will take your heart is a remembrance of, and a relationship with the one and only God that created your heart to be indwelt by Love—tailor made to contain him.

> *My name is Wonderful.*
> *I am your Counselor, I will satisfy your heart—*
> *I really will;*
> *I will reveal myself to you,*
> *I will give you ears to hear*
> *wonderful words that come from my heart*
> *to build you up*
> *in the most holy faith.*

#3   The Wonder of the Incarnation of Jesus Christ

Pr. Tom Schaller:

Most of the religions of the world want us to explain it:

"How could God become a man?"

And we simply say, "We cannot explain it to you. It is a mystery that must be revealed. But if you will allow yourself to believe, you will be in a state of total wonder, and you will worship God who made you in his image, and you will know Him in a personal way—is not that wonderful that you can know God—and He will satisfy your heart because He became a man for your heart.

God is love in action—love rushing on a rescue mission.
He never intended His beloved man to be
lonely and miserable,
wandering in a dark forest.
That is against His Own nature of light.

God took the initiative in Bethlehem when He became
a human being in the Person of Jesus Christ.
He joined us in the darkness of life and said,
"I am the Light of the world."
The dark forest of human existence was lit up.

When Christ lived among men, He knew what poverty was.
He was hungry,
thirsty,
sorrowful,
lonely and tired.
He relieved pain in others,
but He experienced the full force of it Himself.

Christ died on the cross; He bore the shattering responsibility
of guilt.
He lifted the heaviest burden from man's most
sensitive part—his conscience.
He brought peace to his mind by forgiving the
sins which caused the guilt.

Receiving Him is the greatest miracle in life.
Christ called it
"to be born anew."
Paul called it
"to become a new person altogether."

The broken relationship with God is restored.
We are at home with God, and therefore
at home with ourselves,
at home with our fellow men,
and at home in our world.

Festo Kivengere:

What kind of love is this that would leave Heaven to come down to a world inundated with evil, and wickedness, and iniquity, and willingly surrender its life to pay the price death demands for every sin? [(Ro 6:23)]

> *God so loved ME,*
> *that He gave His only begotten Son.*
> *This wonder is so great*
> *as to hold the angels of Heaven*
> *...spellbound with eternal wonder.*

#4. The Wonder of The Cross and Absolute Forgiveness

> *Were you there when they crucified my Lord?*
> *Oooooh!*
> *Sometimes it causes me to*
> *—Tremble—Tremble—Tremble—*
> *Were you there when they crucified...*
> *My LOVE?*

I have often wondered If I were there, what would I see? Would it be just another Roman crucifixion, for they were very common in that age. Would I have seen just another misguided, religious zealot; there is plenty of their kind around in *every* age? Some of them were mocking him saying:

> You who destroy the temple and build it in three days, save yourself! If you are the Son of God, come down from the cross.
>
> Matthew 27:40

> He saved others; himself He cannot save. If he is the King of Israel, let Him now come down from the cross, and we will believe Him. He trusted in God; let Him

247

deliver him now if He will have him; for he said, "I am the Son of God."

Matthew 27:42-43

Then a darkness fell upon all the land round about; it was only mid- afternoon but it was like midnight for three hours, and about the ninth hour Jesus cried out with a loud voice, saying:

Eli, Eli, lama sabachthani?" that is, "My God, my God, why have you forsaken me?" Some of those who stood there, when they heard that, said, "This Man is calling for Elijah!" And someone shouted, "Leave him alone; let's see if Elijah will come to save him!

Matthew 27:46-49

What would my mind be thinking? What would my eyes be seeing? Would I see just another criminal brought to justice; because, crucified on either side of Jesus, was a convicted criminal? (Mt 27:38) I might even have been one of their victims.

Then he died—yielded up his spirit—and suddenly there was a rumbling sound—like distant thunder. The ground began to shake; you could hear bedrock beneath your feet splitting, and a devastating earthquake struck and shook us mightily. In the city there were amazing rumors of graves being opened; people who had been dead for decades were walking around—alive and well— Unbelievable! There was also a rumor that as the High Priest and his entourage stood before the veil of the Temple to enter into the Holy of Holies with the blood offering, the veil was rent from top to bottom—right before their eyes! And even the battle-hardened Roman centurion who drove the nails began to "tremble— tremble—tremble"; and he was heard to say, "Truly; this man was the Son of God!" (Mt 27:54)

The Bible doesn't say it, but I feel certain that this man—the centurion who crucified him—is the first one saved by his literal shed blood; probably the very one who got a "Blood bath" when he thrust the spear into Jesus' side to make sure he was dead. (Jn 19:34) Can it be that this wretched man is the very first New Testament Saint? If so, he surely will be one of the most startling of Heaven's trophies, and all will know that only Love could perform such a merciful wonder. Can you fathom it? The first New Testament saint is the one who drove the nails! Is Love incredible, or what??

I think if I were there to see these things I would have been overwhelmed with amazement and wonder; and I do wonder if what I saw would have been enough to turn my heart to God and believe like that centurion.

Pr. Tom Schaller:

But how can a man who has committed a terrible crime be forgiven? How can it be that a person who has raped, or willfully murdered, or stolen millions, ever be forgiven and restored to a state as though they had never committed even one sin? Think about it; reflect upon it often in your heart, and put yourself out there where it is. It may be that I have done something very, very bad—terrible—but in the mind of God it does not exist. In my heart we want to believe it but so often in our emotions we can't accept it; in my heart I would like to believe but somehow in my morality I say, "It's not fair, I need to pay for my sin! I want to pay for my sin myself!"

But Love says, "Oooooh! No, no, no, no... Please! Let me reveal a wonder, a mystery to you; let me forgive you of your sin, let me take it away by the blood of my Son, let me set you free from yourself, let me teach you who I am—your God—because I am Wonderful."

And we say, "Please, Jesus, refresh me in this truth, for this dull, boring life is not touching me; it's not getting hold of me, there's nothing new under the sun, I'm looking but and I find nothing but vanity of vanities everywhere. The water goes up in the air and becomes clouds, and it comes down again as water, and goes back up in the air again; it's just a cycle. And I feel that I too am nothing but part a cycle."

Samson had his eyes plucked out by the Philistines and was in taken to their milling house where he was harnessed to a millstone like a donkey. (Jd 16:21) He went round, and round, and round for endless, miserable hours, day after day. Have you been there? Going round and round, round and round? Have you asked, "Where are the wonders of this life? Is there any? I'm hungry for something, or someone to quicken my mind, my emotions, and my heart." Have you said it: "Please! Thrill me, open it up to me, show me how awesome it is to be refreshed by Love."

Yes, forgiveness is incredible, amazing, marvelous, and it is; oh, so wonderful! Enjoy it, bask in it, breath it in, and let it refresh your spirit. If you don't like yourself, let the Lord Love you—build yourself up with the wonder of His grace and mercy, and realize this: I am forgiven, my sins are gone forever—even the ones I haven't yet committed—buried in the deepest part of the sea, (Mi 7:19) and removed as far as the east is from the west, (Ps 103:12) where even Omniscience cannot remember them, (He 8:12, 10:17) and my life is brand new—I'm a totally, absolutely, new creation of God. (1Cor 5:17)

Maybe you've not heard this in a fresh way; or maybe you say, "I know that." or "I've heard that before." But my prayer is that every believer will discover the fountain of Love from above; that it would well up in us, that it would flow out from us, from emotions enraptured with the wonder of Love that forgives forever and cannot remember sin anymore. If you haven't experienced this lately, if you're looking for it and can't seem to find it for some reason or other, I'm shouting it from the rooftops:

IT IS THERE!

IT IS AVAILABLE TO ALL WHO WILL RECEIVE IT!

COME!

IT'S FREE!

And I would like someone to do that for me when I'm sitting there daydreaming my life away sometimes— to say: Come on now; let's walk together, let's believe Jesus, let's give him everything in our lives; let's chuck all the reasons, and the feelings, and the emotions, and the poor self image and the sin, and the personal identification; let's chuck it all out the window, and:

Let God love you.
Embrace him, walk by faith with him;
you'll find him to be... Faithful And True
because of Love.

#5   The Wonder of the Resurrection

Pr. Tom Schaller:

Here is a dead man; he died on a cross—crucified— and he is absolutely, totally, completely, really, dead. Now, how can that dead man live? He cannot; there is no possible way. But on the third day after his death, God the Father said to this dead man, "Come up here and sit at my right hand!" and he did!

He left his tomb empty and ascended up into Heaven to be seated at the right hand of God. But some say, "Impossible!! Not so; how can a dead man live?" And we say, *"Yes!! Love lifted him!"*

I was sinking deep in sin;
Far from the peaceful shore;
Very deeply stained within,
Sinking to rise no more;
But the Master of the seas,
Heard my despairing cry,
From the waters lifted me,
Now, safe am I.
Love lifted me——Love lifted me;
When nothing else could help,
Love lifted me.

James Rowe

Love lifted our Lord, and seated him above where he ever lives to make intercession for us [He 7:25] and Love lifted you and I with him. [Ep 2:6] So we lift up our eyes and say I want my life to be filled with wonder, like a little child on Christmas morning; with the tree, and the lights, the tinsel, the candy canes, especially all the toys, and the music, and Mom and Dad laughing...Do you remember what that was like? Do you remember getting a new bicycle and being excited and amazed? Do you remember what it was like to be wonder-stricken on Christmas morning? God doesn't want us to be childish, but He loves our childlikeness and open heartedness to the wonders He scatters around us every day—and there are many, many of them.

Pr. Tom Schaller:

I recently read a story about a little boy in Romania who was born with no arms. A well-to-do family in Connecticut, USA, wanted to adopt and, when they heard about this child, went to meet him when he was only one year old. They shared with his mother, Psalm 139:14, which tells of how we are "fearfully and wonderfully made"—even with no arms; they told her they wanted to adopt her son, to love him, and give him a good life with them. She was poor, and loved the child, but she recognized that they loved him also, and were able to give him many more of the resources he would be desperately needing, so she gave him to them for adoption, and they returned to Connecticut. It was no time at all before he learned to use his feet to hold his spoon and feed himself, and he became a topic of conversation when they went out to eat in restaurants. People marveled at the fascinating skill in his feet, but also his loveable face and sweet personality. When he was eight years old they sent him to a school to learn how to play a musical instrument that could be played with his feet. He chose the cello and, with much patience and dedication by his teacher, became so accomplished with it that he was asked to participate in a recital with other gifted students. He was somewhat insecure about it, but agreed to participate if his teacher would stand beside him as he played, just in case he had a problem; she agreed. On the night of the recital there was a huge audience, and when it was his turn he and his teacher walked out onto the stage with a chair and a large pillow that was put on the floor to support the neck of his cello. When he was set to play his teacher nodded for him to begin. A feeling of wonder filled the room; he hesitated, took a deep breath and began. But the very first note sounded was sour as it could be. He stopped, got all red in the face, shrugged his shoulders, and broke into a huge grin as he looked up at his teacher. She warmly smiled back and nodded for him to begin again; he did and played the entire song flawlessly. When he finished there was a moment of silence as the audience was totally amazed at what they had seen and heard. Then an older student stood up and began to clap; others followed with a standing ovation that went on for a long time. Later his teacher commented that he had never once played that song through without many mistakes.

This is like a picture of Jesus and us as we face an ominous world; we're weak, nervous, frayed and flawed—severely handicapped—but he stands beside us and softly says, "I'm always with you, even to the end of the age." (Mt 28:20) God does not hear the sour notes of our life of sin, he only sees the unflawed music and perfection of the life of His Son in us, and how we serve Him by faith—flawlessly—because He prepared us and equipped us with Love that glorifies Him and never fails. This is good news to us and it is not make-believe; it is a wonderful, absolute truth: Love lifts us up.

But do we see humanity in this picture? Do we see a work of faith and a labor of Love? Do we see the wonder of it all as the love of God is turning curses into blessings? Do we see the miracles of life? Yes, we do when we see a child with a beautiful personality—and a smile to go with it—but no arms, playing a cello with his feet; we experience the wonder of Love and we're encouraged by it because we see hope, even for our own weakness and limitation.

God so loved the world that He gave His only begotten Son; and His love now indwells our heart because we believe; now we are looking for, and seeing something beyond reason, and logic, and even ourselves—the wonder of forgiveness, the wonder of the resurrection of Jesus Christ, and the hope of an eternity with Him. One of the very reasons—but not the only reason—God allows us to experience so much despairing in our hearts is that we might come to Him, receive His love, be forgiven, cast all our cares upon Him, (1Pe 5:7) and be refreshed by the wonder of resurrection life.

When we see the wonder of the ages—the empty tomb of the crucified Christ (Mk 16:6; Lu 24:24; Jn 20:2)— we are encouraged indeed, for we are sure that:

*Immanent death
is our greatest weakness.
And resurrection
is Love's greatest victory*

#6   The Wonder of Pentecost

On the day of Pentecost the promised Holy Spirit (Jo
14:16, 26, 15:26, 16:7, Ac 1:5) came to baptize with *fire.* (Ac 2:1-3) The
instant the Disciples believed (whenever that may have
been) they were born again (Jn 3:3-7) and received a new
heart and a new spirit (Ez 11:19, 36:26)—a literal Love reservoir.
(Ro 5:5) But now the Holy Spirit will come to baptize and fill
them (Ac 2:4)—indwell them, (1CO 3:16) and seal them as God's
own treasured people. (Ep 1:13)

The very next scene in the Bible is amazing and
wonderful: Disciples immediately go out into the streets
of the city to share the Gospel with multitudes from
many different nations, who are gathered in Jerusalem
to celebrate the Pentecost Feast. And people were amazed
that they were hearing, in their own native tongue, what
"unlearned Galileans" were sharing with them (Ac 2:5-13)
as though they were all well educated men—which
they obviously were not—who fluently spoke numerous
languages. This provides us with a wonderful picture of
what the Church is really all about.

The wonder of Pentecost transformed weak-willed,
unlearned, Disciples of Jesus Christ into the Apostles of
the infant Church. They went on to establish it and turn
the world upside down. (Is 24:1, 29:16; Ac 17:6) What was the
secret to their amazing transformation and awesome
power? Love.

God so loves the world that He does not waste
one single second
of the process of getting the Love that is in us,
out of us,
and into all the world.

#7   The Wonder of the Rapture

> But now Christ is risen from the dead, and has become
> the firstfruits of those who have fallen asleep. [21] For since
> by man came death, by man also came the resurrection
> of the dead. [22] For as in Adam all die, even so in Christ
> all shall be made alive. [23] But each one in his own order:
> Christ the firstfruits, afterward those who are Christ's
> at His coming.
>
> 1 Corinthians 15:20-23

The resurrected, living, Lord Jesus Christ is the
firstfruit of resurrection; but what does that mean? He
is the literal firstborn of a new species of humanity,
ascended into eternity in a glorified, human body that
is not subject to the natural laws or physics of a time-
space universe. This is the ultimate destiny of the total
person—body, soul, and spirit—of every believer in him.

> But someone will say, "How are the dead raised up? And
> with what body do they come?" Foolish one, what you
> sow is not made alive unless it dies. And what you sow,
> you do not sow that body that shall be, but mere grain-
> —perhaps wheat or some other grain. But God gives it
> a body as He pleases, and to each seed its own body.
> All flesh is not the same flesh: but there is one kind of
> flesh of men, another flesh of beasts, another of fishes,
> and another of birds. There are also celestial bodies and
> terrestrial bodies; but the glory of the celestial is one,
> and the glory of the terrestrial is another. There is one
> glory of the sun, another glory of the moon, and another
> glory of the stars, for one star differs from another star
> in glory. So also is the resurrection of the dead. The
> body is sown in corruption; it is raised in incorruption,
> it is sown in dishonor, it is raised in glory, it is sown
> in weakness, it is raised in power. It is sown a natural
> body, it is raised a spiritual body. There is a natural
> body, and there is a spiritual body.
>
> Verses 35-44

Our natural body has material essence—time-space,
physical, corruptible nature that must return to the dust.

(Jb 34:15) But it is also the home of our soul and spirit—the spiritual body—the immaterial essence of mankind, which has an incorruptible nature. The spiritual body is released when the physical body dies, and will either sink downward into hell—the temporary holding place for the unsaved, generally believed to be located in the literal bowels of the earth— or it will be escorted by angels upward into Heaven. (Lu 16:22) It is notable that in hell the spiritual body is still captive in a time-space format, even as it was before the death of the body. But in Heaven the spiritual body lives in an eternal format, free from all the laws of natural physics—free indeed. (Jn 8:36) It is notable also that the spiritual body, unlike the time-space body, is immortal. We might say it this way: We will all live forever, it's only a question of where; will we be time-space captives, or will we be inhabitants of eternity with God (Is 57:15) We will know for sure at the instant of death when the spiritual body is released to go either one way or the other as the body is laid to rest in the dust of the earth. Now watch this one:

> Behold, I tell you a mystery: We shall not all sleep, but we shall all be changed in a moment, in the twinkling of an eye, at the last trumpet. For the trumpet will sound, and the dead will be raised incorruptible, and we shall be changed. For this corruptible must put on incorruption, and this mortal must put on immortality. So when this corruptible has put on incorruption, and this mortal has put on immortality, then shall be brought to pass the saying that is written: "Death is swallowed up in victory." "O Death, where is your sting? O Hades, where is your victory?"
>
> Verses 51-54

There is a time of unimaginable tribulation coming upon the earth; God has ordained it for the purpose of shaking the entire world, in one last attempt to save every possible soul that will believe on Him. "...He gave his only begotten Son that whosoever will believe on

Him shall not perish, but have eternal life." and He is not willing that any should perish. [2Pe 3:9] He is also not willing that any who are already believers should experience the tribulation to come; therefore, for us, the rapture of the saints in imminent.

The rapture of the Church will signify the beginning of the time of tribulation, which will culminate with the last, great, war—Armageddon—seven years later! The trumpets of Heaven will sound; the entire world will hear them. Then the dead in Christ shall rise; God will resurrect and call up to Heaven every single molecule of the DNA of every physical body of every believer who has ever been laid to rest, to reunite it with their spiritual bodies. And they will not be ordinary, physical bodies, they will be bodies that are "changed"—glorified—fitted and formatted for eternity—because the corruptible must put on incorruption, and the mortal must put on immortality in order to exist in an eternal order.

Then the saints that remain on earth will also be instantaneously changed—glorified—without ever having to pass through death. In the twinkling of an eye they will be caught up to meet Christ in the clouds. It is the great hope of every believer that they will be so blessed as to be included in this amazing event— the wonder of the Rapture of Christ's Church. What a glorious, wonderful, hallelujah shouting, meeting that's going to be!

All who are so blessed as to be raptured
will be completely
wonderstruck
with the reality and beauty of
our Savior and King,
suddenly
before their very eyes

The Book Of Love

#8   The Wonder of His Second Coming.

> Behold, He is coming with clouds, and every eye will see
> Him, even they who pierced Him. And all the tribes of
> the earth will mourn because of Him. Even so; Amen.
>
> Revelation 1:7

> That at the name of Jesus every knee should bow, of
> those in heaven, and of those on earth, and of those
> under the earth, and [that] every tongue should confess
> that Jesus Christ [is] Lord, to the glory of God the
> Father.
>
> Philippians 2:10-11

There will suddenly be an indescribable, awesome anticipation of ...something in the air; silence will cover the earth, all traffic will come to a screeching halt, the chirping of birds and insects will be silent, the rustle of leaves will not be heard, and the guns and missiles of Armageddon will cease.

Then the sky will be lighted up—from horizon to horizon—with His glory as the veil of eternity is drawn back and Heaven is revealed for all the world to see. (Re 19:11) Can you imagine it—the glory? Every shadow will flee away for the glory of God streams from everywhere. Can you imagine the wonder of it? The intensity, this brilliance and beauty of color has never been seen on Planet Earth; the sound will be as nothing ever heard by human ears; everything and everyone on earth, yes, and even in the earth, will be at a standstill, looking up, enraptured, somehow knowing that the moment of His return is at hand. Then He will appear! THE FAITHFUL AND TRUE, (Re 19:11) THE WORD OF GOD, (Re 19:13) KING OF KINGS AND LORD OF LORDS, (Re 19:16) riding upon a winged, white horse—out of eternity, into time and space on Planet Earth! And He is followed by the armies of Heavenly—the saints, clothed in beautiful, clean, shining, white linen—also riding upon white horses; [Re 19:14] The Bible tells us He will come in the clouds of heaven; [Mt 24:30, 26:64; Mk 13:26, 14:62; Re 1:7] I believe billions, and billions of the saints in white robes, on white horses will actually appear to be those clouds.

And every living soul on earth—saved or unsaved—believing or unbelieving—will be totally, completely wonderstruck! Even unbelieving souls captive in the bowels of the earth—Hades, the place of the dead—will be able to see Him, for the Word of God is this: "*every eye shall see Him*".

He will need no introduction!
Every eye will see him!
Every knee will bow!
Every tongue will confess His Lordship!
to the glory of God the Father. [Ro 14:11; Pp 2:11]

#9   The Wonder of the Millennial Kingdom

With the Second Coming, the inauguration of a 1000-year reign of Christ and his saints on earth is at hand. The tribulation age and the Grace Dispensation ends, the Kingdom Dispensation [Mi 4:1-8] begins. Satan will be chained in hell, [Re 20:1-3] and there will be a separation of the sheep and the goats—the saved and unsaved—of the seven-year, tribulation age. [Mt 25:30-46] Those who are believers will inherit a refurbished earth, a world very much like the ancient Garden of Eden. Those who are not believers will be mercifully slain and their souls will sink into the depths of hell to await the second resurrection, the Great White Throne judgment, [Re 20:11] the second death and the lake of fire. [Re 20:6, 21:8]

Mankind has tried for many millennia to solve the problems of the world and the nations. Nimrod was sure he had the answer; but so was Solomon, and Nebuchadnezzar, and the Caesars, and the Czars, and

Hitler who prophesied that the Third Reich would rule for a thousand years, and he spent the lives of millions of men, women, and children to prove it; but it lasted only for a miserable fourteen years. All these powerful men had a dream and tried to do something about the tragedy and misery of life, but they totally missed the wonder of what God has done, is doing and will do; this also is a great wonder to us.

Our problem is not who rules the world, it is sin ruling the world, and the solution to that problem is Love. If there were another solution to the world's tragedy—the sin problem—God would not have sent His beloved Son. If our good deeds, our wishful thinking, our prayers, our morality, our religious belief, or our anything could solve this problem, then God would not have sent His Son to a Roman cross to shed his blood and die for a world of sin. But there simply is no other solution; therefore, the wicked rule, the people mourn; but when the righteous will rule, the people will rejoice, (Pr 29:2) and when Christ returns it will be so—the Righteous will rule, and His people will rejoice.

The Millennial Kingdom is a truly, wonderful world: There will finally be lasting peace on earth, the government will be a monarchy with the Lord Jesus Christ as its King, and his saints will be his Court. (Re 20:6) His throne will be in Jerusalem, the world Capitol.

> The wolf and the lamb shall feed together, the lion shall eat straw like the ox, and dust shall be the serpent's food. They shall not hurt nor destroy in all my holy mountain," Says the Lord.
>
> Isaiah 65:25

Mankind will live very long lives and foster many children who will grow in grace and in knowledge of the King. It will be illegal to sin; the Kingdom is ruled with a rod of iron. (Re 2:26-27) But very near the end, Satan will be unchained and released from hell, to once again try the hearts of men on earth. And again many are be deceived by his lies as he instigates another global conflict that would destroy the world, but, yet again, God steps in. Hell's horde has Jerusalem and the saints surrounded, "and fire came down from God out of Heavenly, and devoured them." (Re 20:7-10) God will not permit the devil, or even mankind, to destroy the earth; He has reserved this work for Himself alone.

The Millennial Kingdom
—the last divine Dispensation—
will finally settle the very last argument
that God is not precisely who he says He is:
LOVE.

Mankind trying to solve the problems of the Planet without Love is like a fantasy, or a fable, or fiction; but reality is better than fiction. Reading our Bible is wonderful; reality is wonderfully better than fiction because every believer has been given a childlike, new heart that is full of imagination, and wonder, and faith. We look up at the stars and are amazed, we look out over the oceans with awe and are amazed; to Jerusalem and we are amazed, to Bethlehem and we are amazed, to the resurrection and we are amazed, to the Church and we are amazed; we look at ourselves and we are amazed by forgiveness, and we are already looking forward in time to the coming kingdom with wonderful expectation.

> While we look not at the things which are seen, but at the things which are not seen: for the things which are seen are temporal; but the things which are not seen are eternal.
>
> 2 Corinthians 4:18

So much of what we see can steal our wonder:

"Hey! Look at those beautiful buildings!"

"Ummm hmmmmmmm. Wow! They're really tall, aren't they?"

"Hey; will ya look at that bridge over there...how long is that?"

"Yeah; but I've seen that before."

"Whoa! Check out this movie; it's about sexual perversion, adultery, treachery, deception, murder, rape.... Oh, yeah, man; this one has it all!"

"Ummm hmmmm. Sure it does; don't hold your breath. I know all about these things and they're not entertaining to me; they bring nothing at all into my heart that is *reality* and gives birth to *wonder*."

Reality is thrilling as we look not at the things which are seen; we look at things that are wonderful, things that transcend time and space—eternal things. Christ on the throne is wonderful, the virgin birth is wonderful, the incarnation of Truth is wonderful, and the resurrection of the dead is very wonderful. These are things we do not see, but we know they are real; these are things that make our life unique; this is the message we live, and we love it. What does the world have for me? Is it a tall building to look at? a long bridge? an important person? a pile of money? is it fame? or fortune? No way! These things are temporary; there is nothing really wonderful about them.

Pr. Tom Schaller:

The world adulterates your divine design; it mocks you, scorns you, cheats you, and steals your true potential, but when you once set your eyes on Christ— to follow him—you become amazed again, like you were when you were a child, but this amazement is definitely linked with reality, and you exclaim, "Wow! That's it; that's what I want; that's reality, and that's wonderful!"

In Matthew 11:25—we note one of the few times in the New Testament when Jesus is rejoicing—for he was a man of sorrows—but here he is a man that is rejoicing: "At that time Jesus answered and said, "I thank You, Father, Lord of heaven and earth, that you have hidden these things from the wise and prudent and have revealed them to babes."

"Babes"—That's us; people who are amazed at the wonder of it all, people who take it with them wherever they go, and minister to those in need, and say, "It is awesome; It is wonderful that God so loved us that he sent his Son, that whosoever believes on him will not perish but have everlasting life. It is amazing! Wonderful!"

Lord, we love being your little children. May Christ be preached everywhere as we look not at the things that are seen, but at things not seen, (2Co 4:18) for so much of what we see can easily steal the wonders of life.

Wonder is contemplating,
being occupied with amazing mysteries
that Heaven reveals to us as common people,
but not so common at all;
"babes",
because we are uncommonly rich in
wonderful things that are real,
wonderful things are not temporal,
but are eternal.

#10. The Wonder of Heaven

Now I saw a new heaven and a new earth, for the first heaven and the first earth had passed away. Also there was no more sea.

Revelation 21:1

The first heavens, and the first earth is gone; melted, dissolved, and has passed away. [2Pe 3:10, Mi 1:4] And "new" in this verse is translated from the Greek, *kainos*, meaning: a brand new, never before existed, superior creation replacing an inferior old one. But why doesn't God just fix what was already there?   Could God transform the existing, time-space format of the material universe into an eternal format? Absolutely! But it must be that the material universe is destined to somehow become the hellfire, home of the damned—the ultimate, cumulative, lake of fire [Mi 1:3-4; Re 20:10-15]—even an endless, everlasting, *universal black hole*. Horror of horrors!

The essence of this present world is a time-space format, which includes all the restrictions and limitations of time-space physics, but after our resurrection we are in glorified bodies—formatted for the *eternal* order—suited for a life without limits or limitations of any form. How wonderful will that be? to live on a new earth, and have a new, eternal universe for our playground? to have bodies that are not subject to the laws and limits of physics? to finally be out-of-the-box that has held us captive all our lifetime? This is going to be wonderful!

And there will be no more sea because a sea necessarily involves limits; it must be contained, and that demands boundaries and separation which is not consistent with an eternal order.

> And at last, life's voyage o'er,
> Take us to the Heavenly shore,
> Safe in port, to dwell with Thee
> Where there shall be
> "no more sea.
>
> *Henry Coppee, 1887*

Then I, John, saw the holy city, New Jerusalem, coming down out of heaven from God, prepared as a bride adorned for her husband.

Verse 2

When John saw the New Jerusalem he knew, and understood that this was his eternal home. He was totally astonished and wrote about its beauty through no less than seventeen verses of Revelation 20; telling of its size, its shape, its lights, its foundations; its crystal, and gold, and jasper and on, and on, and on. It's as though he just couldn't stop talking about it; we can almost feel his exuberant joy and wonder.

I think it was like that when I first met my wife; she was (and still is) a lovely, beautiful woman, and I knew she was going to be my wife; it was an awesome feeling to be in love. But adorned in her wedding gown with all the frills, smiling as she came down the aisle to meet me at the altar, I must say, she was simply, totally wonderful; I could hardly believe my eyes; I could not stop gazing at her with admiration and desire to be with her forever. So it will be when we see our new home, the New Jerusalem, coming "down the aisle"—out of Heaven, from God to us...adorned with Love.

> And I heard a loud voice from heaven saying, "Behold, the tabernacle of God is with men, and He will dwell with them, and they shall be His people. God Himself will be with them and be their God.
>
> Verse 3

One thing is clear from this wonderful verse: God's desire is—and always has been—to dwell with His people. If you're born-again of the Spirit of God, you are a living Tabernacle, and God is ever present in you. "He inhabits the praises of His people" (Ps 22:3) literally means that God inhabits everything we do to His glory.

Adam and Eve lived in the Garden of Eden, and the presence of God was there, walking with them in the cool of the day. (Ge 3:8) The Israelites lived in a tent, so God said, "Put me in a tent that I may dwell among them!" (Ex 40:32) When His people built the Temple to replace the Tabernacle, God said, "Put me in the Temple now!" (Ps 11:4)

Finally, God said, "Put me in my people so I can be with them all the time! Make them my Tabernacle!" (1Co 16:9)

We have heard it said, "You never really know a person until you live in the same house with them." Experience has taught us that there is a measure of wisdom in those words, but to dwell with Him in His eternal Tabernacle will be an experience wonderful beyond human imagination. We understand what it means to be "His people" but as we dwell with Him in person, in His eternal Tabernacle in Heaven, we will get to know Him within the perspective of in an entirely new dimension: I am my Beloved's; now my Beloved is mine. (Song 2:16, 6:3)

> And God will wipe away every tear from their eyes; there shall be no more death, nor sorrow, nor crying. There shall be no more pain, for the former things have passed away.
>
> Verse 4

One of the most wonderful of promises in the entire Bible is this: "God will wipe away every tear from their eyes..." But what does this mean? He will clear our memory of every single remembrance that does not glorify Him. Because of the blood of the Cross, He has already forgiven and forgotten my sins, buried them in the deepest part of the sea, and remembers them no more; it is as though I had never sinned, as though my sins do not now exist—and really never did. Presently I know they do in my own mind; and if I forget, I'm sure someone could remind me. But when God wipes away every tear, it will be a done deal! Now, even we will not remember any of our sins—not one; or anyone else's for that matter. Hallelujah! We might say it this way: Not one single thing that does not glorify God will enter into Heaven; not a memory, not a thought, not any action or inaction—nothing, no remembrance that can ever in any possible way bring a tear to my eye—will be excluded from this wonderful, precious, promise. I won't even know what happened; but suddenly, instantly my eyes will be opened to the reality of...Love! Ooooh! Praise Jesus forever, and ever, and ever, wonderful world without end. Amen! Hallelujah! As I never before have known it, I will know the truth of this awesome scripture:

> [9] But as it is written: "Eye has not seen, nor ear heard, nor have entered into the heart of man the things which God has prepared for those who love Him."
>
> 1 Corinthians 2:9

The greatest wonders of our Heavenly home have never occurred to the human mind; they are so wonderful as to defy description; no words can truly express their beauty, their grandeur, their design and construct, their meaning or the impact they will have upon our person. But is it not wonderful just to use our imagination on this most amazing topic of the wonders of Love?

No more sin nature,
no more bad memories,
no more pain,
no more tears,
no more sorrow,
no more hospitals,
no more cemeteries,
no more goodbyes,
—AND, WONDER OF WONDERS —
when we see his glory!

ABOUT THE AUTHOR
Pastor Ron Swingle

Pastor Ron has been a disciple and servant of the Lord Jesus Christ since 1977. In 1984 (at age 50) he resigned from his position as a professional, industrial designer, and project engineer with a prominent, Portland cement manufacturing corporation in upstate New York, to become a full-time Bible college student at Stevens School of The Bible in Lenox, MA. He graduated, magna cum laude, from Maryland Bible College & Seminary, in Baltimore, MD in 1988, with an Associate's Degree, and again in 1990 with high honors, and a Bachelor's Degree in Christian Theology. A solo, missionary adventure across Pakistan in 1987, which included the cities of Karachi, Lehore, and Sheikhupura and other towns in the Punjab Province, was the highlight of his Bible College experience. He was ordained in 1991 at the Greater Grace World Outreach (GGWO) annual convention.

A 28-year veteran of GGWO Ministries, he has served on various, outreaches, missions, and Bible study groups. He led a team of experienced evangelists to Baltimore's infamous red-light district (1986-2000), and pastored The Finished Work Church of Towson, MD (1995-2005). His education in engineering-physics and mathematics, in addition to thirty years of design and engineering experience, equips him in a very unique way for ministry. His secular skills, combined with spiritual

271

gifts of love, wisdom, understanding, evangelism, and Christian counseling, integrate with his writing style to produce a highly organized flow of thinking with God in categories of truth.

Pastor Ron is presently with the volunteer staff of GGWO, in Baltimore, MD, and is the Assistant Pastor of Greater Grace Christian Fellowship, a Church-planting adventure in Silver Spring, MD. He devotes much of his spare time to writing blogs for online publication, and has written a number of small, doctrine booklets, but this is his very first, formal publication.